A city of sweet speech scorned,
On whose chill stone
Keats withered, Coleridge pined
And Chatterton,
Beardless with poison, froze.

DANTE GABRIEL ROSSETTI

For the children and their teachers
at Prior Weston School,
Whitecross Street,
London

London

A Collection of Poetry of Place

✳

Edited by
BARNABY ROGERSON

ELAND · LONDON

This arrangement, introduction and biographical
notes © Barnaby Rogerson

ISBN 978 1-903651-03-2

First published in October 2003 by Baring & Rogerson Books,
Eland Publishing Ltd, 61 Exmouth Market,
Clerkenwell, London EC1R 4QL
Second edition published by Eland in 2010

Pages designed and typeset by Antony Gray
Cover design using James Tissot's 'The Thames' (1876)
reproduced by permission of the
Wakefield Art Galleries and Museums.
Printed and bound in Spain by
GraphyCems, Navarra

Contents

Introduction

This collection first arose out of a series of animated conversations with John Symmons. John was the dour, dishevelled gardener who lived in half the old servant's basement in Southside House, Wimbledon. I got to know him gradually, for I spent many a summer working beside him in the walled garden, exchanging little more than grunts as I mixed cement and he cut the lawn by hand. He was a curmudgeonly fellow, but he eventually grew hospitable and would make up big mugs of tea heavily spiked with whisky. No mention was ever made of the hidden ingredient. It was part of the conspiracy of silence that infected all who became involved with this remarkable Jacobean house. John would blame his employer, Major Malcolm Munthe, for having gradually destroyed the garden due to the depredations of the guard dogs. The Major, for his part, sighed for the lost flowerbeds of his youth that had been so lovingly planted by his mother. 'But what can I do?' he would declare, 'with such a useless gardener?' Then he would pull himself together and add, 'though I believe my Mother was fond of John.' After another pause, he would add, 'Well at least he doesn't drink.' You could smell the drink on John's breath at any hour of the day. But since the Major had lost all powers of taste and smell when he was left for dead on the beach of Anzio . . .

It was only after the Major died, and when John was himself very ill, that I got to know him better. He would ask me into his flat, which had not seen a woman, a duster or a mop since he had moved in after the War. The walls were dark with soot and nicotine from his pipe. It was dark but not dirty, like an old black house in the Outer Hebrides. His life was built of tea, tobacco, drink, church architecture and poetry. The latter was his true love. He had an astonishing memory and could quote page after page of verse as well as sprinkling his conversation with *Waste Land* couplets:

> Of Magnus Martyr hold
> Inexplicable splendour of Ionian gold
>
> Flowed up the hill and down King William Street,
> To where Saint Mary Woolnoth kept the hours
>
> To luncheon at the Cannon Street Hotel
> Followed by a weekend at the Metropole.

His poetry books were in his bedroom. There were no rare first editions or inscribed notes, just row after row of well-thumbed paperbacks. He had good taste in coffee and despite the reverence he felt for a Late Norman arch he seemed to possess not a flicker of Christian faith.

His childhood was a locked door. Only the coincidence that my daughter went to school on the old street market where he lived opened a crack into those carefully guarded memories. He came from a large Cockney family. The memory of his brothers seemed to make him wince. Indeed the only humour he retained from this period was the memory of the first of the many, many German bombs that landed on his neighbourhood. According to him the bomb did no damage apart from knocking the head off a statue of Milton outside nearby St Giles'. Sometime later he was evacuated to the safety of a farm in Kent. He harboured idyllic memories of this period and the food and attention that was lavished on him. From this period came his love of gardening and poetry.

I am not certain that he ever went home to his family again. Perhaps they had all perished in the Blitz. He could clearly remember when the grounds of my daughter's school, Prior Weston, which stands in the shadow of the Barbican Centre, was a great stable yard for Whitbread's London brewery. From out of the school gates rumbled the horse-drawn carts that delivered barrels of beer to the pubs of London. According to John the stables were provided with their own 'tap' which flowed freely during working hours.

Long rambling conversations with John identified around half the poems in this collection. Others have come from chance meetings with poets at the bar of Filthy McNasty's on Amwell Street, over coffee at Al's Bar on Exmouth Market or at the dawn end of one of Tchaik and Melissa's parties in their flat in Powis Terrace. Edward Barker, Alan Jenkins, Barry Cole, David Tibet, Mark Valentine, Rodolph de Salis, Peter Ackroyd, Gilbert & George, Matthew Sturgis, Andrew Wilson, Turi Munthe, Alexander Monro, Christopher Logue, Mary Clow and Linda Kelly have all helped make the collection richer than it would have been through their photocopied suggestions, loans, letters and gift of books. Even with their help the collection remains idiosyncratic.

The second edition has been improved thanks to letters sent in by such readers as Dr Ian Blake, Charles Lutyens, Max Dorras, Rodolph de Salis and Peter Matthews (of the Museum of London) who managed tactfully to garland their corrections with praise.

I have arranged the poems chronologically but would have liked to include many more twentieth-century poets. The cumulative cost of permissions has however made this difficult. The most noticeable absences are Louis MacNeice,

Edith Sitwell, Mervyn Peake and great chunks of the London-impregnated verse of T. S. Eliot's *Waste Land*.

The flavour of London brought back from the past by this mass of verse is astonishingly potent. At times it reads like a corrective to political history. Princes are only remembered by their dog's collar, while it is the criminal riding to the gallows, or the forgotten prisoner in the Tower who wins undying fame. Although it offers a stately progress through centuries of evolving taste and culture there is no unifying historical vision, no grand avenue of urban perspective in this tidal valley of mud, gravel, power and gold. Instead you begin to feel that we are all being observed by the unblinking eyes of the poets; touched by God, madness, desire, the modern equivalents of London gin or a lethal combination of them all.

The Ruin

Well-wrought this wall: Weirds broke it.
The stronghold burst . . .

snapped rooftrees, towers fallen,
the work of Giants, the stonesmiths,
mouldereth.

Rime scoureth gatetowers
rime on mortar.

Shattered the showershields, roofs ruined,
age under-ate them.

And the wielders and wrights?
Earthgrip holds them – gone, long gone,
fast in gravesgrasp while fifty fathers
and sons have passed.
Wall stood,
grey lichen, red stone, kings fell often,
stood under storms, high arch crashed –
stands yet the wallstone, hacked by weapons,
by files grim-ground . . .
. . . shone the old skilled work
. . . sank to loam-crust.

Mood quickened mind, and a man of wit,
cunning in rings, bound bravely the wallbase
with iron, a wonder.

Bright were the buildings, halls where springs ran,
high, horngabled, much throng-noise;

these many mead-halls men filled
with loud cheerfulness: Weird changed that.

Came days of pestilence, on all sides men fell dead,
death stretched off the flower of the people;
where they stood to fight, waste places
and on the acropolis, ruins.

Hosts who would build again shrank to the earth.
Therefore are these courts dreary
and that red arch twisteth tiles,
wryeth from roof-ridge, reaching groundwards . . .
Broken blocks . . .

There once many a man
mood-glad, goldbright, of gleams garnished,
flushed with wine-pride, flashing war gear,
gazed on wrought gemstones, on gold, on silver
on wealth held and hoarded, on light-filled amber,
on this bright burg of broad dominion.

Stood stone houses: wide streams welled
hot from the source, and a wall all caught
in its bright bosom, that the baths were
hot at hall's hearth: that was fitting . . .

. . .
Thence hot streams, loosed, ran over hoar stone
unto the ring-tank . . .
. . . It is a kingly thing
. . . city

'The Ruin' survives on two leaves of manuscript that are so badly
scarred by fire that sections of the verse are illegible. This
haunting description of a ruined and deserted Roman city is the

very first English poem. It casts a melancholic mood, looking back to a vanished golden age, a mood that has since become a dominant characteristic of English-ness. It was written perhaps three hundred years after the legions had evacuated the province of Britannia. Many have argued that the ruined city is Aquae Sulis, but Bath was never a walled town. The references to gatetowers and hacked wallstone could refer to London and especially those massive Roman ramparts of flint you can still see near the Barbican. At that time the Saxons dwelt west of The Ruins, in Covent Garden.

London Bridge

London bridge is broken down
Gold is won and bright renown
Shields resounding
War horns sounding
Hildyr shouting in the din
Arrows singing
Mail coast ringing
Odin makes our Olaf win

London Bridge fell in 1014 when Ethelred of England and Olaf of Norway attacked a Danish army camped on the south bank of the river at Southwark. The reference to Odin, the old pagan All-Father and victory-giver, is curious from this avowedly Christian period, though it might be no more than a literary loyalty to the old pagan sagas.

FROM *Chronicle* BY *Richard of Devizes (1180–90)*

I do not at all like that city. All sorts of men crowd together there from every country under the heavens. Each race brings its own vices and its own customs to the city. No one lives in it without falling into some sort of crimes. Every quarter of it abounds in great obscenities . . . Whatever evil or malicious thing that can be found in any part of the world, you will find in that one city. Do not associate with the crowds of pimps, do not mingle with the throngs in the eating-houses; avoid the dice and the gambling, the theatre and the tavern. You will meet with more braggarts than in all France: the number of parasites is infinite . . . jesters, smooth-skinned lads, Moors, flatterers, pretty boys, effeminates, pederasts, singing and dancing girls, quacks, belly-dancers, sorceresses, extortioners, night-wanderers, magicians, mimes, beggars, buffoons: all this tribe fill all the houses. Therefore, if you do not want to dwell with evildoers, do not live in London.

Devizes's damnation provides many of us with as neat a summary of the enduring attractions of our street life as many an earnest ode sung in their praise. It was written when London was under the governance of its very first and its longest reigning Lord Mayor, Henry Fitz Ailwyn, who held office from 1189–1212. Fitz Ailwyn has now been followed by 670 worthy successors who are all sworn into office, processed and feasted on the Day of St Simon and St Jude, which allows for the Lord Mayor's Show to happen at a weekend close to 28th October, a week before our streets whiff of cordite on bonfire night.

FROM *The Canterbury Tales* BY *Geoffrey Chaucer*

> In Southwark at the Tabard as I lay
> Ready to wend on my pilgrimage
> To Canterbury with full devout courage
> At night was come in-to that hostelry
> Wel nine and twenty in a company,
> Of sundry folk, by adventure y-fall
> In fellowship, and pilgrims were they all.
> That toward Canterbury Wolden ride:
> The chambers and the stables were wide,
> And well we were'n esed atte beste

In 1873 the silly fools knocked down the old Tabard Inn on Southwark's Borough High Street where Chaucer had stayed in 1383 on the first leg of his pilgrimage to Canterbury, and where for centuries plays were staged in the courtyard during the Southwark Fair.

Goeffrey Chaucer (1343–1400) knew London as a native. He was also well connected, a friend of the poet John Gower whilst his wife was sister to John of Gaunt's third wife. He held a number of appointments at court – Comptroller of Customs and Subsidy of Wools, Skins and Tanned Hides as well as a two year stint as Clerk of the King's Works to the young Richard II. He survived his master's deposition and in the year of Henry IV's accession took over a house in the garden of the chapel of St Mary next door to Westminster's White Rose Tavern. It was here that he completed the last of the twenty-four *Canterbury Tales*. He was the first to be buried in a corner of nearby Westminster Abbey that would over the centuries become Poets' Corner.

Ring-a ring o'roses

Ring-a ring o'roses
a pocket full of posies
A-tishoo! A-tishoo!
We all fall down.

This rhyme famously alludes to the first signs of Plague infection, a pink coloured rash and a swelling ring (about the size of a nutmeg), while posies – sweet smelling bunches of herbs such as rosemary – were ineffectively carried to shield the disease. A-tishoo recalls the fits of sneezes suffered in the last stages of the disease. The Black Death led to the creation of special pest-houses in Stepney, Soho Fields, Marylebone and the vast plague pit at Cripplegate in the City. The mortality was so great in London amongst the educated classes that it killed off Norman-French which was henceforth replaced by English. One of the safest ways to avoid the infection was to take to the boat villages moored on the Thames, which at one point held ten thousand people. John Taylor, the water poet, wrote:

All trades are dead, or almost out of breath,
But such as live by sickness and by death.

When Adam delved

> When Adam delved, and Eve span,
> Who was then the gentleman?

This immortal rhyme was popularised by John Ball, a vagrant priest who worked with Wat Tyler and Jack Straw to make a common front out of the Peasants' Revolt of 1381. Justice, not loot, drove the rebel bands to liberate the prisons at Marshalsea and Fleet and to burn the legal records stored in Lambeth Palace, the New Temple and the Knights Hospitallers. The rich furnishings, clothes and plate found at John of Gaunt's sumptuous palace of the Savoy were burnt and his jewels were ground into powder before being sprinkled into the Thames.

Wat Tyler's adversary Sir William Walworth was buried in St Michael's Church which was demolished by road widening for London Bridge in 1831. It housed an epitaph.

> Here under lieth a man of Fame,
> William Walworth called by name;
> Fish-monger he was in life-time here,
> And twice Lord Mayor, as in Books appere;
> Who with courage starte, and manly might,
> Slew Wat Tyler, in King Richard's sight.

The rebellion of Jack Cade's Kentish men seized control of the city of London in 1450. William Shakespeare gives Jack Cade a wonderful bacchanalian speech in *Henry IV, Part II*:

> Now is Mortimer lord of this city. And here, sitting upon
> London-stone, I charge and command that, of the city's

cost, the pissing-conduit run nothing but claret wine
this first year of our reign.

The image of the London-stone as a throne-like symbol of
authority is now difficult to recapture. This venerable fragment
was built into the outer southern wall of the church of St
Swithin, Cannon Street but is now embedded in the wall of a
Chinese bank. It is presumed to be an old Roman mile-stone,
though John Michell makes a more tantalising case for it as King
Lud's foundation stone, thereby reviving Geoffrey of Mon-
mouth's poetic dynasty lists.

London Lickpenny

In London there I was bent,
I saw myself, where truth should be atteint,
Fast to Westminster ward I went
To a man of law, to make my complaint;
I said, 'For Mary's sake, that holy saint,
Have pity on the poor that would proceed;
I would give silver, but my purse is faint:
For lack of money I may not speed.

As I thrust throughout the throng
Amongst them all, my hood was gone;
Nathless I let not long
To King's Bench till I come.
Before a judge I kneeled anon,
I prayed for God's sake he would take heed;
Full ruefully to him I gan make my moan:
For lack of money I may not speed.

Beneath him sat clerks, a great rout;
Fast they were written by one assent;
There stood up one, and cried round about,
'Richard, Robert, and one of Kent!'
I wist not well what he meant,
He cried so thike there indeed;
There were strong thieves shamed and shent,
But they that lacked money might not speed.

These are the first three verses from a traditional sixteen-verse ballad, the tale of a fifteenth-century ploughman seeking justice in an exciting, magnetic but disdainful city where only money talks. Sometimes attributed to John Lydgate (1370–1449).

FOUR OF THE SEVEN VERSES FROM
To the City of London
BY *William Dunbar*

London, thou art of townes A *per se*.
  Soveraign of cities, semeliest in sight,
Of high renoun, riches, and royaltie;
  Of lordis, barons, and many goodly knyght;
  Of most delectable lusty ladies bright;
Of famous prelatis in habitis clericall;
  Of merchauntis full of substaunce and myght:
London, thou art the flour of Cities all.

Above all ryvers thy Ryver hath renowne,
  Whose beryall stremys, pleasaunt and preclare,

Under thy lusty wallys renneth down,
  Where many a swanne doth swymme with wyngis fare;
  Where many a barge doth saile, and row with are,
Where many a ship doth rest with toppe-royall.
  O! townes of townes, patrone and not-compare:
London, thou art the flour of Cities all.

Upon thy lusty Brigge of pylers white
  Been merchauntis full royall to behold;
Upon thy sretis goth many a semely knyght
  In velvet gownes and cheynes of fyne gold.
By Julyus Cesar thy Tour founded of old
May be the hous of Mars victoyall,
  Whos artillary with tonge may not be told:
London, thou art the flour of Cities all.

Strong by thy wallis that about the standis;
  Wise by the people that within the dwellis;
Fresh is thy ryver with his lusty strandis;
  Blith be thy chirches, wele sownyng be thy bellis;
  Riche be thy merchauntis in substance that excellis;
Fair be thy wives, right lovesom, white and small;
  Clere be thy virgyns, lusty under kellis:
London, thou art the flour of Cities all.

William Dunbar is thought to have rattled off this salute to the City at a Christmas dinner given in honour of the Scottish Ambassador by the Lord Mayor. The Scottish Embassy was in town to negotiate with Henry VII the marriage of his daughter Princess Margaret Tudor to James IV, so flattery was in the air. Tradition recalls Dunbar as 'a Scottysh preyst sytting at oon of the syde tablys' while the Royal accounts from the year 1501 record a payment of £5 to the Court Poet Dunbar 'eftir he com furth of Ingland'. His unofficial verse is more direct and appealing:

> My head ached last night so that I couldn't write today. The migraine oppresses me so badly, piercing my forehead like a crossbow so that I can hardly look at the light.

And there is his description of courtship:

> His pretty beard was combed and trimmed, but it was spattered with broth, and he was a towny, pushy and foolish. He held her fast, he kissed and fondled her, as if he were over-powered by passion. Yet what he was doing showed that he wanted to fuck.

So it appears that William was the first to use the f-word in literature. He was born in 1465 and was last recorded alive in 1513, the year of the fateful battle of Flodden when the flower of Scotland perished.

Mother Shipton's Prophecy

> Before the geud folk of this Kingdom be undone,
> Shall Highgate Hill stand in the middle of Lundun.

The Magnificat from the Bible
TRANSLATED BY William Tyndale

from the 1526 edition, the Gospel of St Luke, Chapter one

And Elizabeth was filled with the holy goost, and cryed with a loude voyce, and sayde: Blessed arte thou among wemen, and blessed is the frute of thy wombe. And whens hapeneth this to me, that the mother off my lorde shulde come to me? Loo, as sone as the voyce of thy salutacion sownded in myne eares, the babe lepte in my belly for ioye. And blessed arte thou that belevedst, For those thinges shalbe performed which were told the from the lorde.

And Mary sayde. My soule magnifieth the lorde. And my sprete reioyseth in god my savioure, For he hath loked on the povre degre of his hondemayden. Beholde nowe from hensorth shall all generacions call me blessed. For he that is myghty hath done to me greate thinges, and blessed ys his name: And hys mercy is always on them that feare him thorowoute all generacions. He hath shewed strengthe with his arme, he hath scattered them that are proude in the ymmaginacion of their hertes. He hath putt Doune the myghty from their seates, and hath exalted them of lowe degre. He hath filled the hongry with goode thinges: And hath sent awaye the ryche empty. He hath remembred mercy: and hath holpen his servaunt Israhel. Even as he promised oure fathers, Abraham and to his seede forever.

Tyndale left England for Antwerp in the early 1520s after his request to Cuthbert Tunstall, the Bishop of London, for permission to translate the New Testament had been refused. In 1526 the first edition of Tyndale's brand new translation came off the press and sold like hot cakes largely because the Bishop of London's agents were buying up all the copies that they could get their hands on. Judged heretical, they were publicly burned at the back of old St Paul's Cathedral later in the year. (This edition is now so rare that the British Library only recently acquired their copy for a million pounds.) Tyndale was horrified by the book burning though the quick sales provided the immediate finance for a revised edition. Whilst working on the sequel – a translation of the Old Testamant – Tyndale was snatched off the streets of Antwerp by Tudor secret agents working hand-in-hand with officers of the Holy Roman Empire. His last letter, a humble request to the prison governor for a lamp to work by, a cap to keep out the cold and his Hebrew dictionaries, was left unanswered. On the executioner's scaffold Tyndale prayed, 'Lord! open the King of England's eyes'. Within a year the realpolitik of the English Reformation led to the public championing of an English Bible by the very monarch who had arranged for Tyndale's execution.

Tyndale's work lives on, for the thirty scholars commissioned to prepare an English Bible during the reign of King James used Tyndale's work as their crib. That great fountainhead of the English language, the King James Bible, is around two-thirds pure Tyndale.

St Pauls, books and fire

On the exact same spot where the bishop of London had burned Tyndale's bible his successors in political authority would soon advance to the burning of human flesh. Henry VIII executed both Catholics and Protestants to show a balanced mind but during his young son's reign, only Catholics were persecuted. In Mary's reign the tables were turned and it was the Protestants who suffered – as recalled in that endearing Nursery rhyme:

> Mary, Mary quite contrary
> How does your garden grow?
> With cockle shells and silver bells
> And little maids all in a row.

The cockle shells refer to the badge of Catholic pilgrims heading south to the shrine of St James of Compostella in the land of Mary's devout husband, Philip II of Spain. The silver bells are from the new rituals of the Latin mass that came out of the councils of the Catholic Counter-Reformation while the little maids all in a row refer to the scaffolds filled with the dangling corpses of Protestant martyrs, women as well as men. This policy would be energetically reversed by Elizabeth.

As well as death, the book trade had always been associated with St Pauls. Even before Caxton set up his printing press the book dealers worked out of St Pauls, storing their stock in the safety of the subterranean crypts. The Great Fire of 1666 torched the old cathedral and its priceless hoard of medieval documents. When the trade revived after that uniquely destructive inferno of English letters, the principal dealers moved north – just a hundred yards north – to Paternoster Square and Paternoster Row. Here they remained, gradually spreading out to colonise the parish of Clerkenwell with print works, while the neighbouring parish to the west, St Bride's and Fleet Street, was home to the newspapers. This remained so for three centuries until they were burnt out for a second time, by the Blitz.

FROM *Prothalamion* BY *Edmund Spenser*

At length they all to merry London came,
To merry London, my most kindly nurse,
That to me gave this life's first native source,
Though from another place I take thy name,
An house of ancient fame:
There when they came whereas those bricky towers
The which on Thames' broad aged back do ride,
Where now the studious lawyers have their bowers,
Their whilome wont the Templar-knights to bide,
Till they decay'd through pride;
Next whereunto there stands a stately place,
Where oft I gained gifts and goodly grace
Of that great lord, which therein wont to dwell . . .

Edmund Spenser (1552–99) was educated as a 'poor scholar'
at Merchant Taylor's School in London before finishing at
Cambridge. Through a student friendship he gained the
patronage of the Earl of Leicester at whose 'stately place' he
wrote both *The Shepheardes Calendar* and *The Faerie Queen*.
Preferment brought him a post in Ireland, though all his gains
were swept aside by Tyrone's rebellion of 1598. Three weeks
after he escaped back to the safety of London he died.

Oranges and Lemons

Oranges and lemons
Say the bells of St Clement's.
Lend me five farthings
Say the bells of St Martins's.
When will you pay me?
Say the bells of Old Bailey.
When I am rich
Say the bells of Shoreditch.
When will that be?
Say the bells of Stepney.
I'm sure I don't know
Says the big bell of Bow.

Or, as it first appears as *London Bells* printed in 1744 within the covers of *Tom Thumb's Pretty Song Book*, whose 37 jingles were collected together by Mary Cooper.

Two sticks and an apple,
Ring the bells at Whitechapel.

Old Father Bald Pate,
Ring the bells Aldgate.

Maids in white aprons,
Ring the bells at St Catherine's.

Oranges and lemons,
Ring the bells at St Clement's.

When will you pay me?
Ring the bells at the Old Bailey.

When I am rich,
Ring the bells at Fleetditch.

When will that be?
Ring the bells at Stepney.

When I am old,
Rings the great bell at Paul's.

Other variant verses long since purged because of their offensive nature include such lines as:

Blackamoor, Taunymmor, suck a bubby:
Your father's a cuckold, your mother told me.

Lines BY *Thomas Wyatt*

Sir Thomas Wyatt (1503–42), who is credited with introducing the sonnet into England, endured two spells in the Tower. The first was in 1536 when Thomas Cromwell was organising the show trial of Queen Ann Boleyn by torturing confessions of incest from her brother and his friends. The second was in 1540 for suspected 'papist tendencies'. It was during this second period that he composed

They flee from me, that sometime did me seke
With naked fote stalkyng within my chamber.
Once have I seen them gentle, tame, and meke,
That now are wild, and do not once remember
That sometyme they have put them selves in danger,
To take bread at my hand, and now they range,
Busily sekyng in continuall change.

To His Son BY *Walter Raleigh*

Three things there be that prosper up apace
And flourish whilst they grow asunder far,
But on a day, they meet all in one place,
And when they meet, they one another mar;
And they be these – the wood, the weed, the wag.
The wood is that, which makes the gallows-tree,
The weed is that, which strings the hangman's bag,
The wag my pretty knave, betokeneth not,
Green springs the tree, hemp grows, the wag is wild;
But when they meet, it makes the timber rot,
It frets the halter, and it chokes the child.
Then bless thee, and beware, and let us pray,
We part not with thee at this meeting day.

Sir Walter Raleigh (1552–1618) wrote much of his poetry while
a prisoner in the Tower. He was first there in 1592, almost in
sport, for having seduced one of the Queen's maids of honour.
He recovered his situation by composing a long verse ('Cynthia,
the Lady of the Sea') in honour of Queen Elizabeth, and by
marrying his sweetheart. His second imprisonment was during
the reign of James I. It was a political jail sentence, passed in
honour of the Spanish alliance. For twelve years Sir Walter lived
in the Garden House beside the Bloody Tower, where he wrote
his multi-volume *History of the World*, dabbled in scientific
experiments, received guests and invented a warship. He was
released in 1616 to lead an expedition to find El Dorado, and
having failed, was sent back to the Tower and executed.

Elegy For Himself
BY *Chidiock Tichborne*

My prime of youth is but a frost of cares,
My feats of joy is but a dish of pain,
My crop of corn is but a field of tares,
And all my good is but vain hope of gain.
The day is past, and yet I saw no sun,
And now I live, and now my life is done.

My tale was heard and yet it was not told,
My fruit is fallen and yet my leaves are green;
My youth is spent and yet I am not old,
I saw the world and yet I was not seen.
My thread is cut and yet it is not spun,
And now I live, and now my life is done.

I sought my death and found it in my womb,
I looked for life and saw it was a shade;
I trod the earth and knew it was my tomb,
And now I die, and now I was but made.
My glass is full, and now my glass is run,
And now I live, and now my life is done.

As Johnson would attest a couple of centuries later, 'Depend upon it, Sir, when a man knows he is to be hanged in a fortnight, it concentrates his mind wonderfully.' This haunting elegy was written on 19 September 1586 in the Tower of London, the night before Chidiock was hanged for his Catholic sympathies.

Queen Elizabeth's Speech at Tilbury

My loving people, we have been persuaded by some that are careful for our safety, to take heed how we commit ourselves to armed multitudes, for fear of treachery.

But I do assure you, I do not desire to live in distrust of my faithful and loving people. Let tyrants fear. I have always so behaved myself that, under God, I have placed my chiefest strength and safeguard in the loyal hearts and goodwill of my subjects, and therefore I come among you as you see at this time, not for my recreation and disport, but being resolved, in the midst and heat of battle, to live or die amongst you all, to lay down for my God, and for my kingdom, and for my people, my honour and my blood, even in the dust.

I know I have the body of a weak and feeble woman, but I have the heart and stomach of a king, and a king of England too, and think foul scorn that Parma or Spain or any Prince of Europe should dare to invade the borders of my realm, to which, rather than any dishonour shall grow by me, I myself will take up arms, I myself shall be your general, judge and rewarder of every one of your virtues in the field.

Not poetry it is true, but rhetoric with a sting. Delivered by Queen Elizabeth I on 9 August 1588 to her troops massed around the Thames-side fort at Tilbury to defend London from the Spanish Armada.

FROM *Richard III*
BY *William Shakespeare*

Act One, Scene Four. London. The Tower.
Enter CLARENCE *and* KEEPER.

KEEPER Why looks your Grace so heavily to-day?
CLARENCE Oh, I have passed a miserable night,
So full of fearful dreams, of ugly sights,
That as I am a Christian faithful man,
I would not spend another such a night,
Though 'twere to buy a world of happy days,
So full of dismal terror was the time!
KEEPER What was your dream, my lord? I pray you tell me.
CLARENCE Methoughts that I had broken from the Tower . . .

FROM *King Lear*

EDGAR Of Bedlam beggars, who, with roaring voices
Strike in their numb'd and mortified bare arms
Pins, wooden pricks, nailes, sprigs of rosemary

Bedlam was slang for the Bethlehem hospital on Finsbury Circus which cared for the mentally-ill. In 1815 the lunatics (including the visionary fairy painter Richard Dadd) were moved into imposing new premises built for them in Lambeth. These were vacated in 1930 and most suitably transformed into the Imperial War Museum.

All the World's a Stage
by *William Shakespeare*

All the world's a stage,
And all men and women merely players:
They have their exits and their entrances;
And one man in his time plays many parts,
His acts being seven ages. At first the infant,
Mewling and puking in the nurse's arms.
And then the whining schoolboy, with his satchel,
And shining morning face, creeping like snail
Unwillingly to school, and then the lover,
Sighing like a furnace, and with a woeful ballad
made to his mistress' eyebrow. Then a soldier,
Full of strange oaths, and bearded like the pard,
Jealous in honour, sudden and quick in quarrel,
Seeking the bubble reputation
Even in the cannon's mouth. And then the justice,
In fair round belly with good capon lined,
With eyes severe and beard of formal cut,
Full of wise saws and modern instances:
And so he plays his part. The sixth age shifts
Into the lean and slippered pantaloon,
With spectacles on nose, and pouch on side;
His youthful hose, well saved, a world too wide
For his shrunk shank; and his big manly voice,
Turning again toward childish treble, pipes
And whistles in his sound. Last scene of all,
That ends this strange eventful history,
Is second childishness and mere oblivion,
Sans teeth, sans eye, sans taste, sans everything.

For all the world indeed, but first spoken in London and forever associated with The Globe and the other early London stages. William Shakespeare (1564–1616) was born into a prosperous, provincial family from Stratford. Married by the age of eighteen, by the time his first work was published, *Venus and Adonis* in 1593, he had probably already spent ten years knocking around the London stage as an occasional playwright and actor. By 1599 he had made good, was a shareholder in The Globe and thereafter started to expand his property holdings back home in Stratford. The sketchy facts of his bourgeois career fit uneasily with the complicated, sexually ambiguous character who addressed all his sonnets to the youth W. H.

It was only thanks to the chance decision of two old business colleagues, John Heming and Henry Condell, to collect together some dog-eared actors' scripts some six years after his death and put together a memorial edition 'to keep the memory of so worthy a friend and fellow alive' that the world has any record of William Shakespeare.

FROM *The Tragedy of Dr Faustus*
BY *Christopher Marlowe*

Now hast thou but one bare hour to live,
And then thou must be damned perpetually;
Stand still you ever-moving spheres of heaven,
That time may cease, and midnight never come.
Fair nature's eye, rise, rise again and make
Perpetual day, or let this hour be but
A year, a month, a week, a natural day . . .

O I'll leap up to my God: Who pulls me down?
See, see, where Christ's blood streams in the firmament.
One drop would save my soul, half a drop, ah my Christ . . .

These fearful lines are suitable for recital in a Deptford inn such
as the one where Marlowe was murdered one night in 1593. One
witness declared that he was 'stabbed to death by a bawdy
serving-man, a rival of his in lewde love'. Another claimed that
Marlowe had set out to kill a man called Ingram, who only
stabbed him in the eye in self defence. The parish register offers
up yet another version, that he was slain on 1st June by one
Francis Frezer. Marlowe was a free-thinking playwright attached
to the Earl of Nottingham's theatrical company. He may have
been caught up in one of the entrapment plots constantly being
hatched by Queen Elizabeth's secret service. Michael Drayton
(1563–1631) describes in *Of Poets and Poesy* how Marlowe

Had in him those brave translunary things
That the first poets had, his raptures were
All air and fire, which made his verses clear;
For that fine madness still did he retain
Which rightly should possess a poet's brain

FROM *Epithalamion made at Lincolnes Inne*
BY *John Donne*

The Sun-beames in the East are spread,
Leave, leave faire Bride, your solitary bed,
No more shall you returne to it alone,
It nourseth sadnesse, and your bodies print,
Like to a grave, the yielding downe doth dint;
You and your other you meet there anon;
Put forth, put forth that warme balme-breathing thigh,
Which when next time you in these sheets will smother,
There it must meet another.
Which never was, but must be, oft, more nigh;
Come glad from thence, goe gladder than you came,
To day put on perfection, and a woman's name.

Daughters of London, you which bee
Our Golden Mines, and furnish'd Treasurie,
You which are Angels, yet still bring with you
Thousands of Angels on your marriage daies...

This is John Donne, the lusty reprobate of the sunlit afternoon bedroom speaking, the young man who was flung into Fleet prison and sacked from his job as secretary to the Lord Keeper for seducing the daughter of Sir George Moore. It is not the voice of the venerable Dean of St Paul's splicing Jacobean theology with his wit. Thomas Carew (1598–1639) recognized this division in the man with his eulogy to Donne:

Here lies a King that rul'd, as he thought fit
The universal monarchy of wit;
Here lies two Flamens, and both those the best:
Apollo's first, at last the true God's priest.

Life BY *Francis Bacon*

The world's a bubble and the Life of man
Less than a span
In his conception wretched, from the womb
So to the tomb;
Curst from his cradle, and brought up to years
With cares and fears.
Who then to frail mortality shall trust,
But limns on water, or but writes in dust.

Yet whilst with sorrow here we live oppressed,
What life is best?
Courts are but only superficial schools
To dandle fools:
The rural parts are turned into a den
Of savage men:
And where's a city from foul vice so free,
But may be termed the worst of all the three?

Domestic cares afflict the husband's bed,
Or pains his head:
Those that live single take it for a curse
Or do things worse:
Some would have children: those that have them none,
Or wish them gone:
What is it, then, to have, or have no wife,
But single thraldom or a double strife?

But our affections still at home to please
Is a disease:
To cross the seas to any foreign soil,

Perils and toil:
Wars with their noise affright us: when they cease,
We are worse in peace; –
What then remains, but that we still should cry
Not to be born, or being born, to die?

You might read this, the most celebrated of all Francis Bacon's verse, in his observatory tower which survives, with its panelling intact, just to the east of Islington's Canonbury Square. The gardens of Gray's Inn is another place imbued with the spirit of this extraordinary man. He designed these gardens where he would wander, arm in arm, with Raleigh. Bacon fell from his high estate in 1621 when his enemies at court 'squeezed' the Lord Chancellor of his wealth. He was accused of bribery, lodged in the Tower and forced to surrender £40,000.

From this same period – and mood – comes this anonymous verse placed on the water conduit that ran through Cheapside at the time of King James I's visit to the City of London.

Life is a drop, a sparkle, a span,
A bubble: yet how proude is man.
Life is a debt, which, at that day,
The poorest hath enough to pay.
This world's a stage, whereon today,
Kings and meane men parts do play.
Tomorrow others take their roomes,
While they do fill up graves and toomes.

And here's another 'moral rhyme', also put up for King James I but this time on the conduit as it run through Gracechurch Street.

Kingdomes change, worlds decay:
But trueth continues till the last day.
Let money be a slave to thee,
Yet keep this service if you can:
For if thy purse no money have,
Thy person is but half a man.

FROM *The Poly-Olbion* BY *Michael Drayton*

She Peryvale perceiv'd prank'd up with wreaths of wheat,
'why should I not be coy, and of my beauties nice,
Since this my goodly grain is held of greatest price?'

In 1612 the village of Peryvale (now Perivale in west London)
had a reputation for producing the purest grain for the city's
millers. Michael Drayton (1563–1631) was a professional hack
whose commissioned work met with general applause whilst his
cherished labour-of-love, *Poly-Olbion*, was ignored.

London Bridge BY *James Howell*

Where such vast arches he observed that might
  nineteen Rialtos make for depth and height;
When the cerulean God these things survey'd
He shook his trident, and astonished said,
'Let the whole earth now all the wonders count,
This bridge of wonders is the paramount.'

These lines are imitations of a eulogy on Venice composed by
Jacopo Sannazaro, a seventeenth-century Venetian poet.

In Westminster Abbey
BY *Francis Beaumont*

Mortality, behold and fear!
What a change of flesh is here!
Think how many royal bones
Sleep beneath this heap of stones!
Here they lie had realms and lands,
Who now want strength to stir their hands
here from their pulpits sealed with dust
they preach, 'In greatness is no trust.'
Here's an acre sown indeed
with the richest, royall'st seed
That the earth did e'er suck in,
Since the first man died for sin.
Here the bones of birth have cried,
'Though gods they were, as men they died.'
Here are sands, ignoble things,
Dropt from the ruined sides of kings.
Here's a world of pomp and state,
Buried in dust, once dead by fate.

Francis Beaumont (1584–1616) was part of the circle of English
dramatists that collected around Ben Johnson and the Mermaid
Tavern. Beaumont shared his clothes, lodging and even his work
with John Fletcher. Together they created fifty plays.

Thames, the most lov'd of all the Oceans sons,
By his old Sire to his embraces runs,
Hasting to pay his tribute to the Sea,
Like mortal life to meet Eternity.
Though with those streams he no resemblance hold,
Whose foam is Amber, and their gravel Gold;
His genuine, and less guilty wealth t'explore,
Search not his bottom, but survey his shore …

FROM *Drunken Barnaby*
BY *Richard Brathwait*

Thence to Highgate, where I viewed
City I so dearly loved,
And th' Horne of Matriculation
Drunk to th' fresh men of our Nation;
To his memory saluted
Whose branch'd head was last cornuted.
Thence to Hollowell, Mother red cap,
In a troupe of Trulls I did hap;
Whoors of Babylon me impalled,
And me their Adonis called;
With me toy'd they, buss'd me, cull'd me,
But being needy, out they pull'd me.
Thence to Islington at Lion,
Where a juggling I did spy one,

Nimble with his Mates consorting,
Mixing cheating with his sporting;
Creeping into th'Case of's viall
Spoil'd his juggling, made them fly all.
Country left; I in a fury,
To the Axe in Alder-bury
First arriv'd, that place slighted
I at Rose in Holborne lighted . . .

Richard Brathwait (1588–1673), the son of a northern squire, squandered his youth in the taverns and brothels of Cambridge and Oxford, followed by a faltering career in the Inns of Court. After his father's death he returned to the broad acres of his ancestral inheritance. He remained a staunch Royalist throughout the Civil War, one son even following Charles II into exile, while another died fighting Algerine corsairs. 'Drunken Barnaby' was partly written in Latin verse as *'Barnabae Itinerarium'*. It is clearly part autobiographical but is also informed by the roistering career of a bachelor maternal uncle, as well as the *Carmina Burana* and the *Liber Macaronices* written by an errant Benedictine who jumped over the walls of Monte Casino.

The Mother Red Cap remained a favourite haunt of prostitutes for centuries, and was later depicted by Hogarth. Islington's Red Lion pub (though made-over in the 1880s) still flourishes and is the home of an innovative small theatre.

To Althea from Prison
BY *Richard Lovelace*

When Love with unconfined wings
Hovers within my gates,
And to my divine Althea brings
To whisper at the grates;
When I lie tangled in her hair
And fetter'd to her eye,
The Gods that wanton in the air
Know no such liberty.

When flowing cups run swiftly round
With no allaying Thames,
Our careless heads with roses crown'd,
Our hearts with loyal flames;
When thirsty grief in wine we steep,
When healths and draughts go free,
Fishes that tipple in the deep
Know no such liberty.

When (like committed linnets) I
With shriller throat shall sing
The sweetness, mercy, majesty
And glories of my King;
When I shall voice aloud how good
He is, how great should be,
Enlarged winds, that curl the flood,
Know no such liberty.

Stone walls do not a prison make,
Nor iron bars a cage;

Minds innocent and quiet take
That for an hermitage;
If I have freedom in my love
And in my soul am free,
Angels alone, that soar above,
Enjoy such liberty.

Lovelace died in penury off Shoe Lane in 1658.

His Tears to Thamasis
BY Robert Herrick

I send, I send, here my supremest kiss
To thee, my silver-footed Thamasis,
No more shall I re-iterate thy Strand
Whereon so many goodly structures stand;
Nor in the summer's sweeter evenings go
To bathe in thee (as thousands others do).
No more shall I along thy crystal glide,
In barge (with boughs and rushes beautified)
With soft-smooth virgins (for our chaste disport)
To Richmond, Kingston, and to Hampton Court.
Never again shall I with finny oar
Put from, or draw unto thy faithful shore;
And landing here, or safely landing there,
Make way to my beloved Westminster;
Or to the golden Cheapside, where the earth
Of Julia Herrick gave me my birth.
May all clean nymphs and curious water dames,
With swanlike state, float up and down thy streams,

No drought upon thy wanton waters fall
To make them lean, and languishing at all.
No ruffling winds come hither to disease
Thy pure, and silver-wristed Naiades.
Keep up your state, ye streams; and as ye spring,
Never make sick your banks by surfeiting.
Grow young with tides, and though I see you never,
Receive this vow, *So fare ye well for ever.*

Robert Herrick (1591–1674), forever associated with the Arcadian charms of the English countryside, was yet born in London, the son of a goldsmith.

FROM *Ode on Leaving the Great Town*
BY *Thomas Randolph*

Come, spur away,
I have no patience for a longer stay,
But must go down
And leave the chargeable noise of this great town:
I will the country see
Where old simplicity
Tho' hid in grey
Doth look more gay
Than foppery in plush and scarlet clad.
Farewell you city wits, that are
Almost at civil war;
'Tis time that I grow wise when all the world grows mad.

When the Assault was Intended to the City
BY *John Milton*

Captain, or Colonel, or Knight in arms,
Whose chance on these defenceless doors may seize,
If deed of honour did thee ever please,
Guard them, and him within protect from harms.

He can requite thee; for he knows the charms
That call fame on such gentle acts as these,
And he can spread thy name o'er lands and seas,
Whatever clime the sun's bright circle warms.

Lift not thy spear against the Muses' bower:
The great Emathian conqueror bid spare
The house of Pindarus, when temple and tower
Went to the ground: and the repeted air
Of sad Electra's poet had the power
To save the Athenian walls from ruin bare.

The last years of Milton's life, when he composed *Paradise Lost* in total blindness, were spent in a quiet corner of Restoration London. From 1662 until his death in 1674 he lived in a simple terraced house on Bunhill Row (formerly Artillery Row). With the customary respect that the City preserves for the past, the actual house, No. 125, has been demolished. He was buried in St Giles without Cripplegate, a handsome parish church that is now embedded within the grim concrete walkways and battlements of the Barbican Centre.

Wordsworth would later appeal to the shades of the great blind poet:

47

Milton! Thou shouldst be living at this hour:
England hath need of thee: she is a fen
Of stagnant waters: altar, sword and pen,
Fireside, the heroic wealth of hall and bower . . .

Thy soul was like a Star, and dwelt apart:
Thou hadst a voice whose sound was like the sea,
Pure as the naked heavens, majestic, free . . .

As did Shelley:

I dreamed that Milton's spirit rose, and took
From life's green tree his Uranian lute:
And from his touch sweet thunder flowed, and shook
All human things built in contempt of man,
And sanguine thrones and impious altars quaked,
Prisons and citadels . . .

Miller of Wandsworth

Hark the clamour of fife and drum
Three thousand Surreymen marching come
Their van by a snow white banner is lead
And the Miller of Wandsworth he walks at their head.
An humble petition they come to present
At the doors of the houses of Parliament
And the windows fly open to catch up the strain
King Charles! King Charles! shall be brought home again.

An anonymous ballad (perhaps partly composed by Lovelace)
recalling the support for King Charles I offered by the villages of
Surrey in opposition to the determinedly Parliamentarian City of
London.

48

FROM ONE OF *James Shirley's dramas*

The glories of our blood and state,
are shadows, not substantial things,
There is no armour against Fate,
Death lays his icy hand on Kings,
Sceptre and Crown,
Must tumble down,
And in the dust be equal made,
With the poor crooked scythe and spade.

James Shirley (1596–1666) was buried with his wife in St Giles-in-the-Fields, two months after the Great Fire had consumed their house and library. They had been 'overcome with affrightments, disconsolations and other miseries occasioned by that fire and their losses'.

The Lord Mayor's Table
BY *Thomas Jordan*

Let all the Nine Muses lay by their abuses,
Their railing and drolling on tricks of the Strand,
To pen us a ditty in praise of the City,
Their treasure, and pleasure, their pow'r and command.
Their feast, and guest, so temptingly drest,
Their kitchens all kingdoms replenish;
In bountiful bowls they do succour their souls,
With Claret, Canary and Rhenish:
Their lives and wives in plenitude thrive,
They want not for meat nor money;
The Promised Land's in a Londoner's hand,
They wallow in milk and honey.

FROM *Upon the Death of his late Highness the Lord Protector*
BY *Andrew Marvell*

That providence which had so long the care
Of Cromwell's head, and numbered every hair,
Now in itself (the glass where all appears)
Had seen the silence of his golden years:
And thenceforth only did attend to trace
What death might least so fair a life deface . . .

I saw him dead. A leaden slumber lies
And mortal sleep over those wakeful eyes:
Those gentle rays over those wakeful eyes:
Which through his looks that piercing sweetness shed;
That port which so majestic was and strong,
Loose and deprived of vigour, stretched along:
All withered, all discoloured, pale and wan –
How much another thing, nor more that man?
Oh human glory vain, oh death, oh wings,
Oh worthless world, oh transitory things!
Yet dwelt that greatness in his shape decayed,
That still though dead, greater than death he laid;
And in his altered face you something feign
That threatens death he yet will live again.

He nothing common did or mean
Upon that memorable Scene:
But with his keener Eye
The Axe's edge did try:
Nor call'd the Gods with vulgar spight
To vindicate his helpless Right,
But bow'd his comely Head,
Down, as upon a Bed

The poetry of Andrew Marvell (1621–78) often celebrates the great public events of Oliver Cromwell's Protectorate but with a gracious respect for the defeated as in these lines above where the 'He' refers to King Charles I not to the Lord Protector. Most of it was penned in private and published (in *Miscellaneous Poems*) after his death in 1681 by his widow. His epitaph in St Giles, London, cites, 'wit and learning, with a singular penetration and strength of judgement'.

*A poem on St James's Park as lately
improved by His Majesty*
BY *Edmund Waller*

Me thinks I see the love that shall be made,
The Lovers walking in that Amorous shade,
The Gallants dancing by the Rivers side,
They bath in Summer, and in Winter slide.
Methinks I hear the Musick in the boats,
And the loud Eccho which returnes the notes,
Whilst over head a flock of new sprung fowle
Hangs in the aire, and does the Sun controle:
Darkning the aire they hover o'er, and shrowd
The wanton Saylors with a feather'd cloud.
The Ladies angling in the Cristal lake,
Feast on the water with the prey they take.
A thousand Cupids on the billows ride,
And Sea-nymphs enter with the swelling tide.

Edmund Waller (1608–87), a cousin of John Hampden, was
educated at Eton and Cambridge. He married a London heiress
in 1631 and on her death courted another. He cut an unedifying
path through the tortured politics of the Civil War years and was
only saved from the execution block by an abject confession.
This poem is dated to 1661.

An anonymous ditty on the
London Spa at Clerkenwell

Now sweethearts with their sweethearts go
To Islington or London Spa
Some go but just drink the water,
Some for the ale which they like better.

This early advertising jingle survives from *Poor Robin's Almanack* of 1773. In 1685 the enterprising publican of the Fountain Inn found a rich mineral spring in the pub garden. The waters were free to the poor, part of an ancient common law tradition. An elegant garden was arranged around the well of spring water and the 'Spa ale' sold here, brewed from its waters, became popular. A similar commercial venture underpins London's great dance theatre at Sadler's Wells in Clerkenwell. A garden and music hall was first laid out in 1683 by Dick Sadler beside his medicinal well. Here Wordsworth saw 'Singers, Rope-dancers, Giants and Dwarfs, Clowns, Conjurors, Posture Masters, Harlequins' just like any contemporary audience.

Lusts of all Sorts
BY *Henry Vaughan*

written upon a meeting with some friends at the Globe

Should we go now a-wand'ring, we should meet
With catchpoles, whores, and tarts in ev'ry street:
Now when each narrow lane, each nook and cave,
Signposts, and shops, pimp for ev'ry knave,
When riotous sinful plush, and tell-tale spurs
Walk Fleet street and the Strand, when the soft stirs
Of bawdy, ruffled silks turn night to day;
And the loud whip, and coach scolds all the way;
When lust of all sorts, and each itchy blood
From the Tower Wharf to Cymbeline, and Lud,
hunts for a mare, and the tired footman reels
'twixt chairmen, torches and the hackney wheels.

Vauxhall Gardens

Now the summer months come round,
Fun and pleasure will abound,
High and low and great and small,
Run in droves to view Vauxhall.
See the motley crew advance,
Led by folly in the dance,
English, Irish, Spanish, Gaul
Drive like mad to dear Vauxhall.

Each profession, ev'ry trade
Here enjoy refreshing shade,
Empty is the cobbler's stall,
He's gone with tinker to Vauxhall,
Here they drink, and there they cram
Chicken, pasty, beef and ham,
Women squeak and men drunk fall.
Sweet enjoyment of Vauxhall.

An anonymous celebration of 'The New Spring Garden', first opened as a Restoration pleasure garden and later ornamented with Chinese pavilions, ruins, statues, fountains, dark secluded walks, booths for private drinking and open-air theatres. Originally designed to be approached by water-taxi, it was a place of licenced debauch, a place of assignation as well as a setting for public festivals such as the first night of Handel's *Water Music* and an 1827 re-enactment of the Battle of Waterloo. Fittingly there were no less than seven farewell parties before the garden was dismantled and auctioned off for building lots in the summer of 1859. It occupied the quadrant formed by Goding Street, St Oswald's Place, Vauxhall Walk and Kennington Lane but now only survives in the prose of Fielding, Thackeray, Congreve, Vanbrugh, Swift, Fanny Burney, Wycherley and Pepys *Diaries* (see 28 May 1667 and 27 July 1668).

The Bailiff's Daughter of Islington

A TRADITIONAL BALLAD

There was a youth and a well-beloved youth,
And he was a squire's son;
He loved the bailiff's daughter dear,
That lived in Islington.

She was coy, and she would not believe
That he did love her so,
No nor at any time she would
Any countenance to him show.

But when his friends did understand
His fond and foolish mind,
They sent him up to fair London,
An apprentice for to bind.

And when he had been several long years,
And never his love could see:
'Many a tear have I shed for her sake,
When she thought little of me.'

All the maids of Islington
Went forth to sport and play,
All but the bailiff's daughter dear,
She secretly stole away.

She put off her gown of great,
And put on her puggish attire,
She's up to fair London gone,
Her true love to require.

As age went along the road,
The weather being hot and dry,
There was he aware of her true love
At length come riding by.

She stepp'd to him as red as any rose,
Catching hold of his bridle ring:
'Pray you, kind sir, give me one penny,
To ease my weary limb.'

'I prithee, sweet-heart, canst thou tell me
Where that thou wast born?'
'At Islington, kind sir' said she,
'Where I have had many a scorn'

'I prithee, sweet heart, canst thou tell me
Whether thou dost know
The Bailiff's daughter of Islington?'
'She's dead, sir, long ago.'

'Then will I sell my goodly steed,
My saddle and my bow;
I will into some far country,
Where no man doth me know.'

'O stay, O stay, thou goodly youth,
Here she standeth by thy side,
She is alive, she is not dead,
And is ready to be they bride.'

'O farewell grief, and welcome joy,
Ten thousand time therefore:
For now I have seen mine own true love,
That I thought I should hath seen no more!'

FROM *Annus Mirabilis:*
the Year of Wonders, 1666
BY *John Dryden*

Methinks already from this Chymick flame
I see a city of more precious mould,
Rich as the town which gives the *Indies* name,
With silver paved, and all divine with gold.

Already, labouring with a mighty fate,
She shakes the Rubbish from her mounting Brow,
And seems to have renewed her Charter's date,
Which Heaven will to the death of time allow.

More great than human now and more August,
New deified she from her Fires does rise:
Her widening Streets on new Foundations trust,
And, opening, into larger parts she flies.

Before, she like some shepherdess did shew
Who sate to bathe her by a River's side,
Not answering to her fame, but rude and low,
Nor taught the beauteous Arts of Modern pride.

Now like a Maiden Queen, she will behold
From her high turrets hourly suitors come;
The East with incense and the West with gold
Will stand, like Suppliants, to receive her doom.

The silver *Thames*, her own domestick Flood,
Shall bear her Vessels like a sweeping Train,
And often wind (as of his mistress proud,)
With longing eyes to meet her Face again.

Now Day appears, and with the day the King,
Whose early Care had robbed him of his rest.
Far off the Cracks of Falling houses ring,
And Shrieks of Subjects pierce his tender Breast

Those who have none sit round where once it was,
And with full eyes each wonted room require;
Haunting the yet warm ashes of the place,
As murder'd men walk where they did expire.

As a necessary personal corrective to all the elegant Vergilian state propaganda Dryden (1631–1700) also produced some profoundly chilling private verse,

> All, all of a piece throughout;
> Thy chase had a best in view;
> Thy wars brought nothing about,
> Thy lovers were all untrue.
> 'Tis well an old age is out,
> And time to begin a new.

FROM *Clever Tom Clinch Going to be Hanged*
BY *Jonathan Swift*

As clever Tom Clinch, while the Rabble was bawling,
Rode stately through Holbourn to die in his Calling;
He stopt at the *George* for a Bottle of sack,
And promis'd to pay for it when he'd come back.

His waistcoat and Stockings, and Breeches were white,
His Cap had a new Cherry Ribbon to ty't;
The Maids to the Doors and the Balconies ran'
And said, lack-a-day! he's a proper young Man.

Swift describes the route of the condemned from Newgate prison (just north of St Paul's Cathedral) to the Tyburn gallows (Marble Arch) in 1726. Those amongst the condemned who could afford it were traditionally allowed to stop for a glass of sack (or in this case a whole bottle of sherry) delivered to them outside the George and Blue Boar pub at 285 High Holborn. This stopping point has given a whole school of gallows humour to the English language such as 'one for the road' and 'on the wagon'. It is also said that Webster, of *The Duchess of Malfi* fame, developed his obsession with death as if a birthright, for his cartwright father held the contract for carting the condemned to the gallows.

FROM *On Poetry: A Rhapsody*
BY *Jonathan Swift*

Be sure at Will's the following Day,
Lie Snug, and hear what Critiks say.
And if you find the general Vogue
Pronounces you a stupid rogue;
Damns all your Thoughts as low and little,
Sit still, and swallow down your spittle.

. . . Your secret kept, your Poem sunk,
And sent in Quires to line a Trunk;
If still you be dispos'd to rhime,
Go try your hand a second time.
Again you fail, yet Safe's the Word,
Take courage, and attempt a Third.

These lines of advice for a young poet may have come from experience. Jonathan Swift, on coming over to London from Ireland was advised by his relative John Dryden that 'Cousin Swift, you will never be a poet'. This was the period when John Dryden was known as the Monarch of Will's, the coffee-house that was the centre of London literary life and stood in Russell Street. According to Dr Johnson, 'Dryden had a particular chair to himself, which was set by the fire in winter, and was then called his winter chair; and it was carried out for him to balcony in summer, and was then called his summer chair.' It wasn't always that easy. In a nearby alley (Rose Street) Dryden was beaten up on a dark winter's night in 1679 by three toughs hired by Rochester, a rival poet, who had been infuriated by an anonymous satire. Alexander Pope, already crippled as a child,

61

had himself carried to Will's so that he might look upon the 'monarch'. A rival literary set was established at Tom's (at 17 Russell Street) which included Garrick, Dr Johnson and Goldsmith.

Two couplets composed BY Alexander Pope; one for the collar of a dog belonging to Frederick, Prince of Wales in 1737, the other addressed to his own kind

I am his Highness' Dog at Kew;
Pray tell me Sir, whose Dog are you?

While pensive poets painful vigil keep
Sleepless themselves, to give their readers sleep.

Verse BY William Pulteney

Some cry up, Gunnersbury,
For Sion some declare;
And some say that with Chiswick-house
No villa can compare.
But ask the beaux of Middlesex,
If Strawb'ry Hill, if Strawb'ry Hill
Don't bear away the bell?

Here William Pulteney (1674–1764), Earl of Bath, is praising the great houses of west London. Horace Walpole's gothick Strawberry Hill, decorated to give it 'the true rust of the baron's wars', is given primacy. How their ghosts must squirm now that it is a teacher training college.

FROM *Epistle to*
the Right Honourable William Pulteney, Esq
BY *John Gay*

When the sweet-breathing spirit unfolds the buds,
Love flies the dusty town for shady woods.
Then Tottenham fields with roving beauty swarm,
And Hampstead balls the city virgin warm:
Then Chelsea's meads o'erhear perfidious vows,
And the pressed grass defrauds the grazing cows.
'Tis here the same; but in a higher sphere,
For ev'n court ladies sin in open air.
What cit with a gallant would trust his spouse
Beneath the tempting shade of Greenwich boughs?

FROM *About in London*
BY *John Gay*

The seasons operate on ev'ry breast;
'Tis hence that fawns are brisk, and ladies dressed.
When on his box the nodding coachman snores,
And dreams of fancied fares; when tavern doors
The chairman idly crowd; then ne'er refuse
To trust they busy steps in thinner shoes.
But when the swinging signs your ears offend
With creak noise, then rainy clouds impend;
Soon shall the kennels swell with rapid streams;
And rush in muddy torrents to the Thames . . .

John Gay (1685–1732) achieved lasting fame with *The Beggar's Opera*, the idea of which was given to him by Jonathan Swift, who suggested that a pastoral poem based on the notorious Newgate prison might 'make an odd pretty sort of thing'. Gay based the anti-hero of his 'Newgate Pastoral' on the popular real-life villain, Jonathan Wild; he was also the first to write in praise of the beautiful game:

> I spy the furies of the football war:
> The 'prentice quits his shop, to join the crew,
> Increasing crowds the flying game pursue.

FROM *The Distressed Poet*
BY *George Keate*

> Nor here shall the Infection stop:
> Quite from the bottom to the top
> The timbers all shall rot and slacken,
> Their heart decay, their surface blacken;
> All which I easily can master,
> By this most wonder-working plaister,
> Whose fermentation and rank juice
> Shall make what's done of little use.
> Thus I, by slow but sure degrees,
> Will shake this building and his ease,
> And when I've tortured every feeling,
> Sudden shall fall th' Etruscan ceiling;
> The ground with beauteous figures strewing,
> Spreading a dusty cloud of ruin.

George Keate, for whom Robert Adam designed an elegant octagonal room for his house in Charlotte Street (now Bloomsbury Street), was much consumed by the furious irritation he felt for architects, decorators and their workmen. Keate would later sue Robert Adam though he lost the case and was made to pay £163 14s. 4d. in damages. The exact nature of his grievance is unknown.

High Street Kensington
BY *Thomas Tickell*

Where Kensington high o'er the neighb'ring lands
'Midst greens and sweets, a Regal fabrick stands,
And sees each spring, luxuriant in her bowers,
A snow of blossoms, and a wilde of flowers,
The Dames of Britain oft in crowds repair
To gravel walks, and unpolluted air.
Here, while the Town in damps and darkness lies,
They breath in sun-shine, and see azure skies;
Each walk, with robes of various dyes bespread,
Seems from afar a moving Tulip-bed,
Where rich Brocades and glossy Damasks glow,
And Chints, the rival of the show'ry Bow.

Thomas Tickell was born at Bridekirk in Carlisle. His friendship with Joseph Addison gained him government employment and they collaborated on Tickell's translation of the *Iliad* (1715) which was attacked by Pope's satire on Atticus. His finest work is the elegy which he created for his collected edition of Addison's works (1721). 'High Street Kensington' was composed in 1722.

FROM *London* BY *Samuel Johnson*

Tho' grief and fondness in my breast rebel,
When injur'd Thales bids the town farewel,
Yet still my calmer thoughts his choice commend,
(I praise the hermit but regret the friend),
Resolv'd at length, from vice and London far,
To breathe in distant fields a purer air . . .

Here malice, rapine, accident, conspire,
And now a rabble rages, now a fire;
Their ambush here relentless ruffians lay,
And here the fell attorney prowls for prey;
Here falling houses thunder on your head,
And here a female atheist talks you dead . . .

Here let those reign, whom pensions can incite
To vote a patriot black, a courtier white;
Explain their country's dear-bought rights away,
And plead for pirates in the face of day;
With slavish tenets taint our poison'd youth,
And lend a lie the confidence of truth.
Let such raise palaces, and manors buy,
Collect a tax, or farm a lottery;
With warbling eunuchs fill our silenc'd stage,
And lull to servitude a thoughtless age . . .

London, the needy villain's gen'ral home,
The common sewer of Paris and of Rome,
With eager thirst, by folly or by fate,
Sucks in the dregs of each corrupted state . . .

They first invade your table, then your breast;
Explore your secrets with insidious art,
Watch the weak hour, and ransack all the heat;
Then soon your ill-plac'd confidence betray.
By numbers here from shame or censure free
All crimes are safe, but hated poverty.
This, only this, the rigid law pursues;
This, only this, provokes the snarling muse.

And here some offerings from his coffee table or from the *Dictionary*:

I will venture to say, there is more learning and science within the circumference of ten miles from where we now sit, than in all the rest of the kingdom.

When a man is tired of London he is tired of life: for there is in London all that life can afford.

Grub Street – Originally the name of a street near Moorfields in London much inhabited by writers of small histories, dictionaries and temporary poems.

Patron – Commonly a wretch who supports with insolence, and is paid with flattery.

Pension – In England it is generally understood to mean pay given to a state hireling for treason to his country.

Dr Samuel Johnson (1709–84), poet, critic, editor, hack, travel-writer and celebrated creator of the first *Dictionary of the English Language* (1755). He had a genius for friendship and was beloved by Reynolds, Burke, Goldsmith, Charles James Fox and of course his biographer Boswell.

FROM *London Suburbs*
BY *William Cowper*

Suburban villas, highway-side retreats,
That dread th'encroachment of our growing streets,
Tight boxes, nestly sash'd, and in a blaze
With all a July sun's collected rays,
Delight the citizen, who, grasping there,
Breathes clouds of dust, and calls it country air.
Oh sweet retirement, who could balk the thought,
That could afford retirement, or could not?
'Tis such an easy walk, so smooth and straight,
The second milestone fronts the garden gate;
A step if fair, and if a shower approach,
You find safe shelter in the next stage-coach.
There prison'd in a parlour snug and small,
Like bottled wasps upon a southern wall,
The man of bus'ness and his friends compress'd
Forget their labours, and yet find no rest;
But still 'tis rural – trees are to be seen
From ev'ry window, and the fields are green;
Ducks paddle in the pond before the door,
And what could a remoter scene show more?

Where has commerce such a mart,
So rich, so throng'd, so drained, and so supplied
As London, opulent, enlarged, and still Increasing London?

William Cowper (1731–1800) was the delicate and melancholic son of an Anglican rector whose creativity was nurtured by a series of compassionate women, noticeably Mrs Unwin, Lady Hesketh and Lady Austen. He is seen as the poet of the evangelical revival and precursor of Wordsworth.

Henry Wallis's famous portrait of *The Death of Chatterton* (in an attic at 39 Brooke Street) is an iconic image of the indifference of London to literary talent. Thomas Chatterton (1752–70) took his life with a dose of arsenic aged just seventeen, having lasted but four months in the city. His one success, the sale of an operetta, to be sung at the Marylebone Pleasure Gardens, allowed him to send money back to his mother and sister in Bristol and to claim, 'I am quite familiar at the Chapter Coffee House, and know all the geniuses there. A character is unnecessary; an author carries his genius in his pen.' Dante Gabriel Rossetti (1828–82) remembered him in these few lines:

> A city of sweet speech scorned,
> On whose chill stone
> Keats withered, Coleridge pined
> And Chatterton
> Beardless with poison froze.

London
BY *William Blake*

I wander thro' each charter'd street.
Near where the charter'd Thames does flow
And mark in every face I meet
Marks of weakness, marks of woe.

In every cry of every Man.
In every Infants cry of fear
In every voice; in every ban.
The mind-forg'd manacles I hear.

How the Chimney-sweepers cry
Every blackning Church appalls.
And the hapless Soldiers sigh
Runs in blood down Palace walls. *soldiers blood*

But most thro' midnight streets I hear
How the youthful Harlots curse
Blasts the new-born Infants tear
And blights with plagues the Marriage hearse.

The fields from Islington to Marybone,
To Primrose Hill and Saint John's Wood,
Were builded over with pillars of gold;
And there Jerusalem's pillars stood.

Her Little Ones ran on the fields,
The Lamb of God among them seen,
And fair Jerusalem, his Bride,
Among the little meadows green.

Pancras and Kentish town repose
Among her golden pillars high,
Among her golden arches which
Shine upon the starry sky.

The Jews's harp House and the Green Man,
The Ponds where Boys to bathe delight,
The fields of Cows by William's farm,
Shine in Jerusalem's pleasant sight.

London was embedded in William Blake's identity, his heaven as well as his hell. He was born in Soho in 1757, the son of a city hosier, was apprenticed as an engraver in Covent Garden and would die in a two-room attic, a 'squalid place of but two chairs and a bed' in Fountain Court off the Strand in 1827. Even his visionary experiences, most famously seeing 'a tree filled with angels', happened in London at Peckham Rye. Walking expeditions into the countryside led him into the outlying villages of Islington, Dulwich and Marylebone. From his house in Broadwick Street, Soho, he would customarily walk along Oxford Street, up Tottenham Court Road to the junction of New Road (London's first bypass and the lineal ancestor of the six-lane Marylebone Road.) At that time it boasted two rowdy pubs on the city limits, The Adam and Eve and the Farthing Pie House variously recorded by Defoe, Dickens and Hogarth. From there a green road twisted up to the pastoral charms of Highgate and Hampstead and its surrounding farmland. Blake was a voracious reader on the brink of political activism, who applauded the French revolution and supported England's own radicals. His hatred of the establishment was complete and his hymn *The Tyger* can be read as a celebration of the cleansing violence of the masses. He had experienced this power at first hand during the Gordon Riots. On the evening of Tuesday 6 June he was walking along Long Acre when he was swept along into the very front rank of the rioters who stormed the Old Bailey, liberated Newgate prison, looted the wine stores off Fetter Lane and fired a distillery.

LINES BY *Percy Bysshe Shelley*

London; that great sea whose ebb and flow
At once is deaf and loud, and on the shore
Vomits its wrecks, and still howls on for more,
Yet in its depths what treasures!

Hell is a city much like London –
A populous and a smoky city.

Epitaph for a Goldfinch

Where Raleigh pin'd within a prison's gloom
I cheerful sung, nor murmur'd at my doom.
But death, more gentle than the law's decree,
Hath paid my ransom from captivity.

This verse was found scratched into the stone wall of the Beachamp Tower in the Tower of London. Below it were the additional words, 'buried, June 23, 1794, by a fellow prisoner in the Tower of London'.

LINES BY *Leigh Hunt*

Leigh Hunt famously staged 'the immortal dinner' when, in March 1817, he entertained both Keats and Shelley at 15 Lisson Grove. Later that year, in December, the painter Benjamin Haydon brought together Charles Lamb, Keats and Wordsworth round one table at 116 Lisson Grove. Here Hunt sings of Hampstead.

A steeple issuing from a leafy rise,
With balmy fields in front, and sloping green,
Dear Hampstead, is thy southern face serene,
Silently smiling on approaching eyes.
Within, thine ever-shifting looks surprise,
Streets, hills and dells, trees overhead now seen,
Now down below, with smoking roofs between –
A village revelling in varieties.

London from Westminster Bridge
BY *William Wordsworth*

Earth has not anything to show more fair:
Dull would he be of soul who could pass by
A sight so touching in its majesty:
This City doth like a garment wear
The beauty of the morning: silent, bare,
Ships, towers, domes, theatres, and temples lie
Open unto the fields, and to the sky,
All bright and glittering in the smokeless air.
Never did sun more beautifully steep
In his first splendour valley, rock, or hill;
Ne'er saw I, never felt, a calm so deep!
The river glideth at his own sweet will:
Dear God! the very houses seem asleep;
And all that mighty heart is lying still!

It is a pleasant irony that the most famous poem in praise of
London was written in the ecstatic exhilaration of leaving the
city at dawn. Wordsworth gives us precise details, 'written on
the roof of a coach, on my way to France, 3rd September 1802'.
It is no longer possible to catch his vista, the London County
Council building now dominates the southern shore and the old
eighteenth-century bridge has long since been replaced. *London,
MDCCCII* gives a much clearer vision of his distaste for the
values of the city, reiterated in these lines from *The Prelude*:

74

                              Private courts,
Gloomy as coffins, and unsightly Lanes
Thrill'd by some female Vendor's scream, belike
The very shrillest of all London Cries,
May then entangle us awhile;
Conducted through those labyrinths, unawares.

London, MDCCCII
BY *William Wordsworth*

O, Friend! I know not which way I must look
For comfort, being, as I am opprest
To think that now our life is only drest
For show; mean handi-work of craftsman, cook,

Or groom – We must run glittering like a brook
In the open sunshine, or we are unblest;
The wealthiest man among us is the best:
No grandeur now in nature or in book

Delights us. Rapine, avarice, expense,
This is idolatory; and these we adore:
Plain living and high thinking are no more;

The homely beauty of the good old cause
Is gone; our peace, our fearful innocence,
And pure religion breathing household laws.

FROM *On First Looking into Chapman's Homer*
BY *John Keats*

Much have I travell'd in the realms of gold,
And many goodly states and kingdoms seen;
Round many western islands have I been
Which bards in fealty to Apollo hold.
Oft of one wide expanse had I been told
That deep-brow'd Homer ruled as his demesne;
Yet did I never breathe its pure serene
Till I heard Chapman speak out loud and bold:
Then felt I like some watcher of the skies
When a new planet swims into his ken;
Or like stout Cortez when with eagle eyes
He star'd at the Pacific – and all his men
Look'd at each other with a wild surmise –
Silent upon a peak in Darien.

Composed by John Keats (1795–1821) at dawn in October 1816 as he walked back home to Southwark having sat up all night with his friend and former schoolteacher, Charles Cowden Clarke, who lived in Clerkenwell. They had been excitedly reading George Chapman's new translation of Homer.

In 1817 he lodged at 76 Cheapside while training to be a surgeon at Guy's Hospital. This was just a short stroll from the site of the Mermaid Tavern, on the junction of Cheapside and Bread Street, used by John Donne, Ben Jonson and William Shakespeare.

Lines on the Mermaid Tavern
BY *John Keats*

Souls of poets dead and gone
What Elysium have you known
Happy field or mossy cavern
Choicer than the Mermaid tavern?
Have you tippled drink more fine
Than mine host's Canary Wine?
Or are the fruits of Paradise
Sweeter than those dainty pies
Of venison?

I have heard that on a day
Mine host's sign-board flew away,
Nobody knew wither, till
An astrologer's old quill
To a sheepskin gave the story,
Said he saw you in your glory,
Underneath a new-old sign
Sipping beverage divine,
And pledging with contented smack
The Mermaid in the Zodiac.

Ode to a Nightingale
BY *John Keats*

My heart aches, and a drowsy numbness pains
My sense, as though of hemlock I had drunk,
Or emptied some dull opiate to the drains
One minute past, and Lethe-wards had sunk:
'Tis not through envy of thy happy lot,
But being too happy in thine happiness –
That thou, light-winged Dryad of the trees,
  In some melodious plot
Of beechen green, and shadows numberless,
Singest of summer in full-throated ease.

O, for a draught of vintage! That hath been
Cooled a long age in the deep-delved earth,
Tasting of Flora and the country-green,
Dance, and Provencal song and sunburnt mirth!
O for a beaker full of the warm South,
Full of the true, the blushful Hippocrene,
With beaded bubbles winking at the brim,
  And purple-stained mouth,
That I might drink, and leave the world unseen,
And with thee fade away into the forest dim:

Fade far away, dissolve, and quite forget
What thou among the leaves hast never known,
The weariness, the fever, and the fret
Here, where men sit and hear each other groan;
Where palsy shakes a few, sad, last grey hairs,
Where youth grows pale, and spectre-thin, and dies;

Where but to think is to be full of sorrow
And leaden-eyed despairs;
Where beauty cannot keep her lustrous eyes,
Or new Love pine at them beyond to-morrow.

Away! Away! For I will fly to thee,
Not charioted by Bacchus and his pards,
But on the viewless wings of Poesy,
Though the dull brain perplexes and retards.
Already with thee! Tender is the night,
And haply the Queen-Mother is on her throne,
Clustered around by all her starry Fays;
But here there is no light,
Save what from heaven is with the breezes blown
Through verdurous glooms and winding mossy ways.

I cannot see what flowers are at my feet,
Nor what soft incense hangs upon the boughs,
But, in embalmed darkness, guess each sweet
Wherewith the seasonable month endows
The grass, the thicket, and the fruit tree wild;
White hawthorn, and the pastoral eglantine;
Fast fading violets covered up in leaves;
And mid-May's eldest child,
The coming musk-rose, full of dewy wine,
The murmurous haunt of flies on summer eves.

Darkling I listen; and for many a time
I have been half in love with easeful Death,
Called him soft names in many a mused rhyme,
To take into the air my quiet breath;
Now more than ever seems it rich to die,
To cease upon the midnight with no pain,

While thou art pouring forth thy soul abroad
In such an ecstasy!
Still wouldst thou sing, and I have ears in vain –
To thy high requiem become a sod.

Thou was not born for death, immortal Bird!
No hungry generations tread thee down;
The voice I hear this passing night was heard
In ancient days by emperor and clown:
Perhaps the self-same song that found a path
Through the sad heart of Ruth, when sick for home,
She stood in tears amid the alien corn;
The same that oft-times hath
Charmed magic casements, opening on the foam
Of perilous seas, in faery lands forlorn.

Forlorn! the very word is like a bell
To toll me back from thee to my sole self!
Adieu! The fancy cannot cheat so well
As she is famed to do, deceiving elf.
Adieu! Adieu! Thy plaintive anthem fades
Past the near meadows, over the still stream,
Up the hill-side; and now 'tis buried deep
In the next valley-glades:
Was it a vision, or a waking dream?
Fled is that music – Do I wake or sleep?

Composed on April 30th under a plum tree in the walled garden
of a graceful little house in Hampstead. Keats's beloved Fanny
dwelt with her family in one half whilst he and his friend Brown
lived in the other. It was not only Keats that was in love; Brown
was obsessed with their young Irish maid. Brown's claret cellar
in Wentworth House has often been thought of as the source of

the Bacchic imagery in the *Ode*, though Robert Gittings brushes these literal readings aside in his biography and speaks of the 'landscape of the mind' and echoes of Dryden and Chaucer. Twenty years later Brown would recall how he first discovered the almost illegible *Ode* scribbled across four or five scraps of paper that had been absent-mindedly tucked into the back of a book that morning.

All on that Magic List Depends
BY *Henry Lutterell*

All on that magic list depends;
Fame, fortune, fashion, lovers, friends:
'Tis that which gratifies or vexes
All ranks, all ages, and both sexes.
If once to Almack's you belong,
Like monarchs, you can do no wrong;
But banished thence on Wednesday night,
By Jove you can do nothing right.

This is testament to the binding power of Almack's Assembly Rooms in King Street, St James's. Almack's reigned over London's high society from 1770–1835. The guest list to the weekly ball was scrutinised by seven dowagers. Men had to dance in breeches (not trousers) and wear white cravats.

Piccadilly
BY *Fredrick Locker*

Piccadilly! Shops, palaces, bustle and breeze
The whirring of wheels, and the murmur of trees;
By night or by day, whether noisy or stilly,
Whatever my mood is, I love Piccadilly.

Wet nights, when the gas on the pavement is streaming,
And young love is watching, and old Love is dreaming,
And beauty is whirling to conquest, where shrilly
Cremona makes nimble thy toes, Piccadilly!

Bright days, when a stroll is my afternoon wont,
And I meet all the people I do know, or don't: –
Here is jolly old Brown, and his fair daughter Lillie –
No wonder some pilgrims affect Piccadilly!

See yonder pair riding, how fondly they saunter,
She smiles on her poet, whose heart's in a canter!
Some envy her spouse, and some cover her filly,
He envies them both, – he's an ass, Piccadilly!

Were I such a bride, with a slave at my feet,
I would choose me a house in my favourite street;
Yes or no – I would carry my point, willy-nilly:
If 'no', – pick a quarrel; if 'yes', – Piccadilly!

From Primrose balcony, long ages ago,
'Old Q.' sat at gaze, – who now passes below?
A frolicsome statesman, the Man of the Day;
A laughing philosopher, gallant and gay;

Never darling of fortune be more manfully trod,
Full of years, full of fame, and the world at his nod:
Can the thought reach his heart, and then leave it
                                    more chilly –
'Old P. or Old Q., – I must quit Piccadilly'?

Life is chequer'd; a patchwork of smiles and frowns;
We value its ups, let us muse on its downs;
There's a side that is bright, it will then turn us t'other,
One turn, if a good one, deserves yet another.
These downs are delightful, these ups are not hilly, –
Let us turn one more turn ere we quit Piccadilly.

Piccadilly! Shops, palaces, bustle, and breeze,
The whirring of wheels, and the murmur of trees;
By night or by day, whether noisy or stilly,
Whatever my mood is, I love Piccadilly.

Frederick Locker-Lampson (1821–95) was born in London from
a naval background. He worked for the Admiralty but left five
years before publishing *London Lyrics* (1857).

Lines Written in Kensington Gardens
BY *Matthew Arnold*

In this lone, open glade I lie,
Screen'd by deep boughs on either hand;
And at its end, to stay the eye,
Those black-crown'd, red-boled pine-trees stand!

Birds here make song, each bird has his,
Across the girdling city's hum.
How green under the boughs it is!
How thick the tremulous sheep-cries come!

In the huge world, which roars hard by,
Be others happy if they can!
But in my helpless cradle I
Was breathed on by the rural Pan!

Calm soul of all things! make it mine
To feel, amid the city's jar,
That there abides a peace of thine,
Man did not make, and cannot mar!

Matthew Arnold was tall with black hair, blue eyes and a commanding presence, made even more formidable by his short-sightedness though all who knew him well considered him the most genial and amiable of men. In 1868 he decided to move away from the social distractions of central London to care better for his invalid son. He was fated to bury two of his sons from this new home at Byron House, the High Street, Harrow.

FROM *Mr Molony's Account of the Crystal Palace*
BY *W. M. Thackeray*

With ganial foire
Thransfuse me loyre,
Ye sacred nymphs of Pindus,
The whole I sing
That wondthrous thing,
The Palace made of windows!
Say, Paxton, truth,
Thou wondrthous youth,
What sthroke of art celistial,
What power was lint
You to invint
this combination cristial

O would before
That Thomas Moores,
Likewise the late Lord Boyron,
Thim aigles sthrong
Of godlike song,
Cast oi on that cast oiron!

And saw thim walls,
And glittering halls,
Thim rising slendther columns,
Which I, poor pote,
Could not denote,
No, not in twinty vollums.

My Muse's words
is like the birds
That roosts beneath the panes there;

Her wings she spoils
'Gainst them brightly iles,
And cracks her silly brains there.

This Palace tall,
This Cristial Hall,
Which Imperors might covet,
Stands in High Park
Like Noah's Ark,
A rainbow bint above it.

The towers and fanes,
In other scaynes,
The fame of this will undo,
Saint Paul's big doom,
Saint Payther's Room,
And Dublin's proud Rotundo . . .

. . . and on and on rolls William Makepeace Thackeray's mock heroic Irish tribute to Crystal Palace as published in Punch in 1851. We have long lost the thrill that previous generations got out of memorized verse. I witnessed an example of this skill last year when an old Somali poet visited our office to buy books. As a young man studying to become an Imam he had been taught in the traditional way, which was to recite the whole Qur'an off by heart. This ability never left him but he found that this facility, once developed, needed exercising. After he had mastered English it seemed perfectly natural for him to memorise a book that he currently admired, which was Bertrand Russell's *Autobiography*. I listened in astonishment as it poured from his mouth, in perfect cadence and pronunciation.

Fog BY *Charles Dickens*

Fog everywhere. Fog up the river, where it flows among green aits and meadows; fog down the river, where it rolls defiled among the tiers of shipping, and the waterside pollutions of a great (and dirty) city. Fog on the Essex marshes, fog on the Kentish heights. Fog creeping into the cabooses of collier-brigs; fog lying out on the yards, and hovering in the rigging of great ships; fog drooping on the gunwales of barges and small boats. Fog in the eyes and throats of ancient Greenwich pensioners, wheezing by the firesides of their wards; fog in the stem and bowl of the afternoon pipe of the wrathful skipper, down in his close cabin; fog cruelly pinching the toes and fingers of his shivering little 'prentice boy on deck. Chance people on the bridges peeping over the parapets into a nether sky of fog, with fog all round them, as if they were up in a balloon, and hanging in the misty clouds.

The London so vividly portrayed by Charles Dickens has also effectively colonised the world's imagination, freezing the city in a mid-nineteenth-century time frame. Foreign visitors are often restless until they can catch a glimpse of this world of spectral fogs, dark gas-lit alleys and creaking tumbledown old houses. Dickens, with his early experience of theatre and journalism, always wrote with a well-tuned ear for the public reading of his works. I feel that he would have been able to recite 'Fog' without so much as a glance at the text of *Bleak House*.

The Waterman
BY *Charles Dibdin*

And did you not hear of a jolly young waterman,
Who at Blackfriars Bridge used for to ply;
And he feather'd his oars with such skill and dexterity,
Winning each heart, and delighting each eye.
He loo'd so neat, and he row'd so steadily:
The maidens all flock'd in his boat so readily,
And he ey'd the young rogues with so charming an air,
That this waterman ne'er was in want of a fare.

Charles Dibdin (1745–1814) was a dramatist, and is said to have
written over twelve hundred songs, including 'Tom Bowling'.

The Embankment
the fantasy of a fallen gentleman on a cold, bitter night
ANONYMOUS

Once in a finesse of fiddles found I ecstasy,
In a flash of gold heels on the hard pavement.
Now see I
That warmth's the very stuff of poesy.
Oh, God, make small
The old star-eaten blanket of the sky,
That I may fold it round me and in comfort lie.

A Ballad of London
BY *Richard Le Galliene*

Ah, London! London! our delight,
Great flower that opens but at night,
Great City of the midnight sun,
Whose day begins when day is done.

Lamp after lamp against the sky
Opens a sudden beaming eye,
Leaping alight on either hand,
The iron lilies of the Strand.

Like dragonflies, the hansoms hover,
With jewelled eyes, to catch the lover,
The streets are full of lights and loves,
Soft gowns, and flutter of soiled doves.

Upon thy petals butterflies,
But at thy root, some say, there lies
A world of weeping trodden things,
Poor worms that have not eye or wings.

From out of corruption of their woe
Springs this bright flower that charms us so,
Men die and rot deep out of sight
To keep this jungle-flower bright.

Paris and London, World-Flowers twain
Wherewith the World-Tree blooms again,
Since Time have gathered Babylon
And withered Rome still withers on.

Sidon and Tyre were such as ye,
How bright they shone upon the tree!
But Time hath gathered, both are gone,
And no man sails to Babylon.

Ah, London! London! our delight,
For thee, too, the eternal night,
And Circe Paris hath no charm
To stay Time's unrelenting arm.

Time and his moths shall eat up all.
Your chiming towers proud and tall,
He shall most utterly abase,
And set a desert in their place.

[Handwritten annotations: "Gods who turned people into animals"; "Paris transforms people into animals."; "Circe Paris" underlined; "Normal insect"; "moths shall eat up" underlined; "Time"; "He"; "London will die out"]

Richard Le Gallienne was born in 1866 in Liverpool where his
father, descended from an old Channel Island family, was the
manager of a brewery. Having failed at accountancy, his beauty
(he was compared to Botticelli's Lorenzo) allied to quick wit
allowed him to charm his way into the heart of literary London,
taking up strategic posts as a reviewer and publisher's reader
interspersed by stints on the stage. In 1891 he married Mildred,
a pretty waitress from his hometown, though she died three
years later during childbirth. His daughter, from a second
marriage, described her father as being split between 'the Bishop
and the Daymon' – one gentle, wise and loving-kind, the other
violently alive, brilliant, cruel, fascinating and dangerous.

Impression de Nuit
BY *Alfred Douglas*

See what a mass of gems the city wears
Upon her broad live bosom! row on row
Rubies and emeralds and sapphires glow.
See! that huge circle, like a necklace, stares
With thousands of bold eyes to heaven, and dares
The golden stars to dim the maps below,
And in the mirror of the mire I know
The moon has left her image unawares.

That's the great town at night: I see her breasts,
Prick'd out with lamps they stand like huge black towers,
I think they move! I hear her panting breath.
And that's her head where the tiara rests.
And in her brain, through lanes as dark as death,
men creep like thoughts . . . The lamps are like pale flowers.

Alfred Douglas was born in 1870, the third son of John Sholto Douglas, defined by Oscar Wilde as the screaming scarlet Marquess. The central love affair of Lord Alfred Douglas's life began in 1891 when his friend from Oxford, Lionel Johnson, took him to have tea with Oscar Wilde at 16 Tite Street. 'I was then twenty years old. Oscar took a violent fancy to me at sight.' Oscar described him 'like a narcissus . . . so white and gold . . . I worship him' though later he would know that 'boys, brandy and betting monopolise his soul'. It was not quite true. Douglas published half a dozen collections of poems, tried marriage for five years and in 1911 became a Roman Catholic. It was he, not Oscar Wilde, that coined the line, 'I am the Love that dare not speak its name'.

Symphony in Yellow
BY *Oscar Wilde*

An omnibus across the bridge
Crawls like a yellow butterfly,
And, here and there, a passer-by
Shows like a little restless midge.

Big barges full of yellow hay
Are moored against the shadowy wharf,
And, like a yellow silken scarf,
the thick fog hangs along the quay.

The yellow leaves begin to fade
And flutter from the Temple elms,
And at my feet the pale green Thames
Lies like a rod of rippled jade.

Oscar Fingal O'Flahertie Wills Wilde was born in Dublin in 1854, the younger son of a celebrated Irish surgeon. After winning the Newdigate Prize in Oxford with his poem *Ravenna* in 1878, he published his first book of poems in 1881, in a limited edition with a binding of gold smeared in tired purple. He became an international figure through his plays, novels, stories, wit and public lectures. His house in Tite Street, complete with devoted wife and two children, was at the centre of London literary life in the 1890s. His immortality was also assured by his love for Lord Alfred Douglas which ultimately led to a civil court case, followed by a trial for sodomy and a prison sentence. His most acclaimed poem, *The Ballad of Reading Gaol*, was composed out of this 'martyrdom' in 1896. After his release from goal he lived as an exile abroad, broken in spirit, wealth and health. He died penniless in Paris in 1900. Though now a humanist martyr, he is not always treated with absolute reverence.

> When Oscar came to join his God,
> Not earth to earth, but sod to sod,
> It was for sinners such as this
> Hell was created bottomless.

City Nights BY *Arthur Symons*

The grey and misty night,
Slim trees that hold the night among
Their branches, and, along
The vague Embankment, light on light.

The sudden, racing lights!
I can just hear, distinct, aloof,
The gaily clattering hoof
Beating the rhythm of festive nights.

The gardens to the weeping moon
Sigh back the breath of tears.
O the refrain of years on years
'Neath the weeping moon!

FROM *London Nights*
BY *Arthur Symons*

The shadow of the gaslit wings,
Come softly crawling down our way:
Before the curtain someone sings,
The music comes from far away:
I stand beside you in the wings…

The little bedroom papered red,
The gas's faint malodorous light,
And one beside me in the bed,
Who chatters, chatters, half the night.

Arthur Symons was born in Milford Haven in 1865, the son of a Cornish Methodist Minister. In his last book of verse, *Jezebel Mort*, he would write, 'Bone by bone, blood by blood, I am a "Cornishman".' As a child he escaped out of his despised surroundings of 'common-place, middle-class people' into the world of language and music. He forged a literary career for himself as a translator, critic and poet but, from 1893, he was possessed by a destructive affair with Bianca, a young chorus girl from the Empire Theatre who is frequently alluded to in *London Nights*. In 1908 he had a complete nervous breakdown in Italy and was certified insane.

In St James's Park, a prose poem
BY *Hubert Crackanthorpe*

A sullen glow throbs overhead; golden will-o-wisps are
threading their shadowy groupings of gaunt-limbed
trees; and the dull, distant rumour of feverish London
waits on the still, night air. The lights of Hyde Park
Corner blaze like some monster, gilded constellation,
shaming the dingy stars; and across the East there
flares a sky-sign – a gaudy crimson arabesque . . . .
And all the air hangs draped in the mysterious,
sumptuous splendour of a murky London night . . .

Hubert Crackanthorpe (1870–96) founded a literary journal,
The Albemarle, which brought together such major figures of
1890's London as Lionel Johnson, Ernest Dowson, James
Whistler and Walter Sickert. He became notorious for the gritty
realism of his short stories, consciously modelled on such free-
thinkers as Emile Zola. He was drowned in the swollen waters of
the Seine aged twenty-six.

London BY *James Whistler*

The evening mist clothes the riverside with poetry, as
with a veil, and the poor buildings lose themselves in the
dim sky, and the tall chimneys become campanili, and
the warehouses are palaces in the night, and the whole
city hangs in the heavens, and fairyland is before us.

Vesperal BY *Ernest Dowson*

Strange grows the river on the sunless evenings!
The river comforts me, grown spectral, vague and dumb:
Long was the day; at last the consoling shadows come:
Sufficient for the day are the day's evil things!

Labour and longing and despair the long day brings;
Patient till evening men watch the sun go west:
Deferred, expected night at last brings sleep and rest:
Sufficient for the day are the day's evil things!

At last the tranquil Angelus of evening rings
Night's curtain down for comfort and oblivion
Of all the vanities observed by the sun:
Sufficient for the day are the day's evil things!

So, some time, when the last of our evenings
Crowneth memorially the last of all our days,
Not loth to take his poppies man goes down and says,
'Sufficient for the day are the day's evil things!'

Ernest Dowson was born in Lee, Kent in 1867, the son of an East End dry-dock owner. Le Galliene remembers him as a 'frail appealing figure, with an almost painfully sensitive face, delicate as a silverpoint, recalling at once Shelley and Keats, too worn for one so young'. Wilde found him 'persistently and perversely wonderful' and Yeats described him as 'gentle, affectionate, drifting'. He died in the house of his friend Robert Sherard at Catford in February 1900 and was buried in the Roman Catholic cemetery at Lewisham.

Dowson also wrote a number of verses 'After Verlaine' – a tribute to Paul Verlaine's abiding influence on the Decadent London poets of the 1890s. Verlaine abandoned wife, mother and infant son to live as an exile in London with Arthur Rimbaud: the dishevelled, absinthe-drinking, hashish- and opium-smoking *enfant terrible*. From September 1872 they lodged at 34 Howland Street off Tottenham Court Road and would later live together at 8 Great College Street in Camden Town. They made use of the library of the British Museum, took long walks out to the suburbs and docks but centred their existence in Soho, then a quarter of radicals and French and Italian exiles. Certain images from this London period (which ended suddenly in July 1873 with yet another pointless alcoholic row) float through into some of Rimbaud's writing. In Brussels Verlaine would fire two shots at Rimbaud.

FROM *Vagabonds* BY *Arthur Rimbaud*

My pathetic brother! What dreadful nights he caused me. 'The whole business never meant much to me; I was playing on his weakness; it was my fault that he would return to exile, to "enslavement" '. He thought that I was strangely jinxed, that I was strangely innocent, and he had other unpleasant ideas as well. I answered this satanic doctor with a sneer . . . Almost every night, as soon as I fell asleep, my poor brother would get up, his mouth stinking, his eyes on stalks – it was just as he dreamed it – and drag me out into the room, yelling in the idiotic anger of his dream.

FROM *Villes* BY *Arthur Rimbaud*

I am an ephemeral and not at all too discontented citizen of a metropolis thought to be modern because every known taste has been avoided in the furnishing and the facades of the houses as well as in the layout of the city. Here you cannot point out the trace of a single monument to the past . . . From my window I see new phantoms roaming through the thick, unrelenting coal-smoke . . . Death without tears, our captive daughter and servant, a desperate Love and a pretty crime whimpering in the mud of the street.

FROM *Métropolitan* BY *Arthur Rimbaud*

From the indigo strait to the seas of Ossian, on pink and orange sands washed by a wine-coloured sky, great avenues of crystal have risen and crossed, inhabited by a swarm of poor young families who buy their food at the fruit stalls. Don't expect riches. This is the city.

From the desert of bitumen flee in headlong flight under blankets of fog smeared over in frightful layers in the sky which curves and unbends, recedes and descends, formed of the most intense and sinister black smoke that the Ocean in the morning can produce, helmets, wheels, little boats and horses' rumps . . .

London BY *John Davidson*

Athwart the sky a lowly sigh
   From west to east the sweet wind carried;
The suns stood still on Primrose Hill;
   His light in all the city tarried:
The clouds on viewless columns bloomed
Like smouldering lilies unconsumed.

'Oh sweetheart, see! How shadowy,
   Of some occult magician's rearing,
Or swung in space of heaven's grace
   Dissolving, dimly reappearing,
Afloat upon ethereal tides
St Paul's above the city rides!'

A rumour broke through the thin smoke
   Enwreathing abbey, tower, and palace,
The parks, squares, the thoroughfares,
   The million-peopled lanes and alleys,
An ever-muttering prisoned storm,
The heart of London beating warm.

John Davidson was born at Barrhead, Renfrewshire, in 1857. He
adored his mother but reviled his father who was a Church
Minister. Forced to leave school aged thirteen to work in the
chemical laboratory of a sugar factory, he yet persevered with his
education. In 1889 he followed his friend, Professor John Nicol,
to London, where he prospered writing ballads and songs.
Described by Richard Le Gallienne as 'rocky and stubborn and
full of Scotch fight' he delighted in contrasting his stalwart

atheism and physical vigour with the languid, well-educated gentility of the English poets. He championed Nietzsche's philosophy but by 1907 his righteous fury had degenerated into a rant. On the 23rd March he sent his last manuscript to his publisher and then waded into the sea.

By the Statue of King Charles
at Charing Cross
BY *Lionel Johnson*

Sombre and rich, the skies;
Great glooms, and starry plains.
Gently the night wind sighs;
Else a vast silence reigns.

The splendid silence clings
Around me: and around
The saddest of all kings
Crowned, and again discrowned.

Comely and calm, he rides
Hard by his own Whitehall:
Only the night wind glides:
No crowds, nor rebels, brawl.

Gone, to his Court; and yet,
The stars his courtiers are:
Stars in their station set;
And every wandering star.

Alone he rides, alone,
The fair and fatal king:
Dark night is all his own,
That strange and solemn thing.

Which are more full of fate:
The stars; or those sad eyes?
Which are more still and great:
Those brows; or the dark skies?

Although his whole heart yearn
In passionate tragedy:
Never was face so stern
With sweet austerity.

Vanquished in life, his death
By beauty made amends:
The passing of his breath
Won his defeated ends.

Brief life, and hapless? Nay:
Through death, life grew sublime.
Speak after sentence? Yea:
And to the end of time.

Armoured he rides, his head
bare to the stars of doom:
He triumphs now, the dead,
Beholding London's gloom.

Our wearier spirit faints,
Vexed in the world's employ:
His soul was of the saints;
And art to him was joy.

King, tried in fires of woe!
Men hunger for thy grace:
And through the night I go,
Loving thy mournful face.

Yet, when the city sleeps;
When all the cries are still:
The stars and heavenly deeps
Work out a perfect will.

To Merry London BY *Lionel Johnson*

Let others chaunt a country praise,
Fair rivers walks and meadow ways;
Dearer to me my sounding days
In London town:
To me the tumult of the street
Is no less music, than the sweet
Surge of the wind among the wheat,
By dale or down.

Lionel Johnson was born at Broadstairs in Kent in 1867, a diminutive, ethereal creature with a pallid, beautiful face. His parents were proud of their Celtic ancestry but were totally English in culture, indeed Anglicans with strong High Church convictions. Lionel was educated at Winchester and New College, Oxford, passing through a number of the higher atheisms before returning to his childhood enthusiasm for the priesthood. In London he dwelt in a succession of rented chambers in the Inns of Court. In the romantic setting of St Ethelreda's Church he was received into the Roman Catholic Church on St Alban's day in 1891. Despite being acknowledged as the best-read and most knowledgeable literary journalist of his day, his character was unravelled by the drink with which he repressed his sexuality. By 1902 he had drunk himself to death.

By the Statue of King Charles at Charing Cross perfectly combines his characteristic cold precision with an unearthly quest after romantic heroes from the past. It was a passion shared by the court poet Edmund Waller, who in 1674 wrote,

> That the First Charles does here in triumph ride,
> See his son reign'd where he a martyr died.

A London Fete BY Coventry Patmore

All night hammers, shock on shock;
With echoes Newgate's granite clanged:
The scaffold built, at eight o'clock
They brought the man out to be hanged.
Then came from all the people there
A single cry, that shook the air;
Mothers held up their babes to see,
Who spread their hands, and crowed with glee;
Here a girl from her vesture tore
A rag to wave with, and joined the roar;
There a man, with yelling tired,
Stopped, and the culprit's crime inquired;
A sot, blow the doomed man dumb,
Bawled his health in the world to come;
These blasphemed and fought for places;
These, half-crushed, with frantic faces,
To windows, where, in freedom sweet,
Others enjoyed the wicked treat.
At last, the show's black crisis pended;

Struggles for better standings ended;
The rabble's lips no longer cursed,
But stood agape with horrid thirst;
Thousands of breasts beat horrid hope;
Thousands of eyeballs, lit with hell,
Burnt one way all, to see the rope
Unslacken as the platform fell.
The rope flew tight; and then the roar
Burst forth afresh; less loud, but more
Confused and affrighting than before.
A few harsh tongues for ever led
The common din, the chaos of noises,
But ear could not catch what they said.
As when the realm of the damned rejoices
At winning a soul to its will,
That clatter and clangor of hateful voices
Sickened and stunned the air, until
The dangling corpse hung straight and still.
The show complete, the pleasure past,
The solid masses loosened fast:
A thief sunk off, with ample spoil,
To ply elsewhere his daily toil;
A baby strung its doll to a stick;
A mother praised the pretty trick;
Two children caught and hanged a cat;
Two friends walked on, in lively chat;
And two, who had disputed places,
Went forth to fight, with murderous faces.

Coventry Patmore (1823–96) was born in Woodford, Essex and
became a convert to Catholicism after the death of his first wife.

Sir Christopher Wren
BY *E. Clerihew Bentley*

Sir Christopher Wren
Said, 'I am going to dine with some men.
If anybody calls
Say I am designing St Paul's.'

Pall Mall BY *Douglas Goldring*

I love to think of bland Pall Mall
(Where Charles made love to pretty Nell)
And rich South Audley Street, and Wapping,
And Bond Street, and the Christmas shopping.
Knightsbridge, the Inner Circle train,
And Piccadilly and Park Lane.

One night of London mist and flame
A corner boy who looked like my
Lover came up and asked my name
But what I saw in that one's eye
Made me lower mine in shame

I followed this young dog who hands
In pockets whistled as he went
That street became the Red Sea sands
Open for him the Jews and meant
To drown me Pharaoh all my bands

Let those piled bricks fall ton on ton
If I did not love you then
I am a King of Egypt's son
His sister-Queen and all their men
If you are not the only one

At a corner of the street
That burned with all its signs alight
Like sores that fogs and acids eat
In old housefronts that weep all night
Like him but for her faltering feet

It was her utterly inhuman
Look the scar across her neck
Came out of this pub drunk that woman
Just as I saw the final wreck
Of human love and all that's human . . .

The Baroque Symbolist poet Guillame Apollinaire was born in Rome in 1880, the child of Olga Kostrowitsky, an aristocratic Polish adventuress and Flugi d'Aspermont, an officer in the Bourbon army. Educated in the south of France, his precocious talent was recognized in a succession of scholarships and prizes. An early champion of the Cubist movement, friend to Braque, Matisse, Picasso, Dufy, Rousseau and lover of Marie Laurencin, he enlisted to fight for France in the First World War. He was horribly wounded in 1916 when a shell-splinter pierced his skull, just eight days after he had been formally granted French citizenship. He died, aged thirty-eight, from the influenza epidemic that swept through Europe in the winter of 1918.

Envoi BY *Ernest Rhys*

Wales England wed; so I was bred. 'Twas merry London
                                        gave me breath.
I dreamt of love, and fame: I strove. But Ireland taught
                                        me love was best:
And Irish eyes, and London cries, and streams of Wales
                                        may tell the rest.
What more than these I ask'd of Life I am content to
                                        have from Death.

At Lord's by *Francis Thompson*

It is little I repair to the matches of the Southron folk,
Though my own red roses there may blow;
It is little I repair to the matches of the Southron folk,
Though the red roses crest the caps, I know.
For the field is full of shades as I near the shadowy coast,
And a ghostly batsmen plays to the bowling of a ghost,
And I look through my tears on a soundless-clapping host
As the run-stealers flicker to and fro,
To and fro: –
O my Hornby and my Barlow long ago!

The Lancastrian poet (1859–1907) here uses the setting
of London's most famous cricket ground to dream of
past heroes and his native county.

from *Embankment at Night*
by *D. H. Lawrence*

At Charing Cross, here, beneath the bridge
Sleep in a row the outcasts,
Packed in a line with their heads against the wall.
Their feet in a broken ridge
Stretched out on the way, and a lout casts
A look as stands on the edge of this naked stall.

One heaped mound
Of a woman's knees

As she thrusts them upward under the ruffled skirt –
And a curious dearth of sound
In the presence of these
Wastrels that sleep on the flagstones without any hurt.

David Herbert Lawrence was born in 1885, the son of a Nottingham miner. A travel-writer and a renowned novelist, his unwittingly controversial works such as *Sons and Lovers*, *The Rainbow*, *Women in Love* and *Lady Chatterley's Lover*, have been immensely influential. However he may yet be better remembered by posterity for his verse. His collected poems were published in 1928; he died in 1930.

Ballad of the Londoner
BY *James Elroy Flecker*

Evening falls on the smoky walls,
And the railings drip with rain,
And I will cross the old river
To see my girl again.

The great and solemn-gliding tram,
Love's still-mysterious car,
Has many a light of gold and white,
And a single dark red-star.

I know a garden in a street
Which no one ever knew;
I know a rose beyond the Thames,
Where flowers are pale and few.

The Ballad of Camden Town
BY *James Elroy Flecker*

I walked with Maisie long years back
The streets of Camden Town,
I splendid in my suit of black,
And she divine in brown.

Hers was a proud and noble face,
A secret heart, and eyes
Like water in a lonely place
Beneath unclouded skies.

A bed, a chest, a faded mat,
And broken chairs a few,
Were all we had to grace our flat
In Hazel Avenue.

But I could walk to Hampstead Heath,
And crown her head with daisies,
And watch the streaming world beneath,
And men with other Maisies.

When I was ill and she was pale
And empty stood our store,
She left the latchkey on its nail,
And saw me nevermore.

Perhaps she cast herself away
Lest both of us should drown:
Perhaps she feared to die, as they
Who die in Camden Town.

What came of her? The bitter nights
Destroy the rose and lily,
And souls are lost among the lights
Of painted Piccadilly.

What came of her? The river flows
So deep and wide and stilly,
And waits to catch the fallen rose
And clasp the broken lily.

I dream she dwells in London still
And breathes the evening air,
And often walk to Primrose Hill,
And hope to meet her there.

Once more together we will live,
For I will find her yet:
I have so little to forgive:
So much, I can't forget.

James Elroy Flecker was born in 1884. After a brief stint as a teacher, he re-trained for the Consular Service and studied Oriental languages at Cambridge. He would be posted to Istanbul, Izmir (old Smyrna) and Beirut before he died, aged thirty.

The Garret BY *Ezra Pound*

Come, let us pity those who are better off than we are.
Come, my friend, and remember
    that the rich have butlers and no friends,
And we have friends and no butlers.
Come, let us pity the married and the unmarried.

Dawn enters with little feet
    like a gilded Pavlova,
And I am near my desire.
Nor has life in it aught better
Than this hour of clear coolness,
    the hour of waking together.

The Garden BY *Ezra Pound*

En robe de parade – SAMAIN

Like a skein of loose silk blown against a wall
She walks by the railing of a path in Kensington Gardens,
And she is dying piece-meal
    of a sort of emotional anaemia.

And round about there is a rabble
Of the filthy, sturdy, unkillable infants of the very poor.
They shall inherit the earth.

In her is the end of breeding.
Her boredom is exquisite and excessive.
She would like some one to speak to her,
And is almost afraid that I
    Will commit that indiscretion.

Ezra Pound (1885–1972), the genius from Idaho, stands as a Janus-like gateway into the English poetry of the twentieth century. In 1909, shortly after he left America, he moved into a first-floor flat at 10 Kensington Church Walk. This was to be his base for five years, from where he befriended W. B. Yeats, whom he nicknamed 'Uncle William', was visited by T. S. Eliot (the other American emigrant who helped to redefine English verse) and from where he would fall in love with Dorothy Shakespear. Ezra entranced the introverted London literary world gathered at such salons as that of Violet Hunt and her lover Ford Madox Ford (where Thomas Hardy, Henry James and Hugh Walpole had been lionized). Pound was observed there wearing trousers made from green billiard-table cloth, vermillion socks, a turquoise ear-ring and a huge tie that had been hand-painted by a Japanese futurist. In the 1920s Pound moved to Paris where, arguably, he wrote his best short poem:

In a Station of the Metro
The apparition of those faces in the crowd:
Petals on a wet, black bough.

From France he moved on to Italy. He was imprisoned for treason by American troops in 1945, having made a series of pro-Fascist broadcasts from Rome during the war. At first he was confined in an outdoor cage at Pisa before he was locked up in an insane asylum in Washington for thirteen years. After his release he returned to Italy and would die in Venice. As he wrote in 'To Whistler':

You and Abe Lincoln from that mass of dolts
Show us there's a chance at least of winning through.

London Revisited BY *Kathleen Raine*

Haunting these shattered walls, hung with our past,
That no electron and sun can pierce,
We visit rooms in dreams
Where we ourselves are ghosts.

There is no foothold for our solid world,
No hanging Babylon for the certain mind
In rooms tattered by wind, wept on by rain.

Wild as the tomb, wild as the mountainside,
A storm of hours has shaken the fine-spun world,
Tearing away our palaces, our faces, and our days.

K. R. Raine was born in 1908 and she saw her first collection of
poems published in 1943. As co-founder of *Temenos* she is often
associated with such fellow seekers after the divine as Cecil
Collins and Philip Sherrard.

Slough BY *John Betjeman*

Come, friendly bombs, and fall on Slough
It isn't fit for humans now,
There isn't grass to graze a cow
Swarm over, Death!

Come, bombs, and blow to smithereens
Those air-conditioned, bright canteens,
Tinned fruit, tinned meat, tinned milk, tinned beans
Tinned minds, tinned breath.

Mess up the mess they call a town –
A house for ninety-seven down
And once a week a half-a-crown
For twenty years,

And get that man with double chin
Who'll always cheat and always win,
Who washes his repulsive skin
In women's tears,

And smash his desk of polished oak
And smash his hands so used to stroke
And stop his boring dirty joke
And make him yell.

But spare the bald young clerks who add
The profits of the stinking cad;
It's not their fault that they are mad,
They've tasted Hell.

It's not their fault they do not know
The birdsong from the radio,
It's not their fault they often go
To Maidenhead

And talk of sports and makes of cars
In various bogus Tudor bars
And daren't look up and see the stars
But belch instead.

In labour-saving homes, with care
Their wives frizz out peroxide hair
And dry it in synthetic air
And paint their nails.

Come friendly bombs, and fall on Slough
To get it ready for the plough.
The cabbages are coming now;
The earth exhales.

In Westminster Abbey BY John Betjeman

Let me take this other glove off
As the vox humana swells,
And the beauteous fields of Eden
Bask beneath the Abbey bells.
Here, where England's statesmen lie,
Listen to a lady's cry.

Gracious Lord, oh bomb the Germans.
Spare their women for Thy Sake,
And if that is not too easy
We will pardon Thy Mistake.
But, gracious Lord, whate'er shall be,
Don't let anyone bomb me.

Keep our Empire undismembered
Guide our Force by Thy Hand,
Gallant black from far Jamaica,
Honduras and Togoland;
Protect them Lord in all their fights,
And, even more, protect the whites.

Think of what our Nation stands for,
Books from Boots' and country lanes,
Free speech, free passes, class distinction,
Democracy and proper drains.

Lord, put beneath Thy special care
One-eighty-nine Cadogan Square.

Although dear Lord I am a sinner,
I have done no major crime;
Now I'll come to Evening Service
Whenever I have the time.
So, Lord, reserve for me a crown,
And do not let my shares go down.

I will labour for Thy Kingdom,
Help our lads to win the war,
Send white feather to the cowards
Join the Women's Army Corps,
Then wash the Steps around Thy Throne
In the Eternal Safety Zone.

Now I feel a little better,
What a treat to hear Thy Word,
Where the bones of leading statesmen,
Have so far been interr'd.
And now, dear Lord, I cannot wait
Because I have a luncheon date.

Monody on the Death of Aldersgate Street Station BY *John Betjeman*

Snow falls in the buffet of Aldersgate station,
Soot hangs in the tunnel in clouds of steam.
City of London! Before the next desecration
Let your steepled forest of churches be my theme.

Sunday Silence! With every street a dead street,
Alley and courtyard empty and cobbled mews,
Till 'tingle tangle' the bell of St Mildred's Bread Street
Summoned the sermon taster to high box pews,

And neighbouring towers and spirelets joined the ringing
With answering echoes from heavy commercial walls
Till all were drowned as the sailing clouds went singing
On the roaring flood of a twelve-voiced peal from Paul's.

Then would the years fall off and Thames run slowly;
Out into the marshy meadow-land flowed the Fleet:
And the walled-in City of London, smelly and holy,
Had a tinkling mass house in every cavernous street.

The bells rang down and in St Michael Paternoster
Would take me into its darkness from College Hill,
Or Christ Church Newgate Street (with St Leonard Foster)
Would be late for matins and ringing insistent still.

Last of the east wall sculpture, a cherub gazes
On broken arches, rosebay, bracken and dock,
Where once I heard the roll of the Prayer Book phrases
And the sumptuous tick of the old west gallery clock.

Snow falls in the buffet of Aldersgate station,
Toiling and doomed from Moorgate Street puffs the train,
For us of the steam and the gas-light, the lost generation,
The new white cliffs of the City are built in vain.

Even as a student Maurice Bowra noticed that, 'Betjeman has a mind of extraordinary originality; there is no one else remotely like him'. John Sparrow could see that, 'plainly what inspired the writer of these stanzas was a sense of place . . . he is not a nature poet, like Wordsworth, but a landscape poet'. Betjeman shared with Dr Johnson a passionate attachment to the Church of England though this faith did not heal his fear of death or erode a dark melancholic streak. He was a loving chronicler of the fabric of London and helped lead the post-war conservation movement, that begun with the lost struggle for old Euston and won a victory with the saving of half of old Spitalfields.

We have not the resources to print T. S. Eliot's *The Waste Land* in this collection. It is however a truly epic London poem, rich in physical, historical and literary references to the City. To read through just verse III, 'The Fire Sermon', brings up flickering references from Shakespeare, Verlaine, Goldsmith and St Augustine cut through with borrowed lines from Spenser such as 'Sweet Thames, run softly, till I end my song'.

Fortunately I cannot read it without being thrown back to my first hearing, performed on the broken stage of the East End's oldest music hall. A naked light bulb and a leaking roof, dripping into a zinc pail, were the sole distractions from the potent lines.

London Airport
BY *Christopher Logue*

Last night in London Airport
I saw a wooden bin
labelled UNWANTED LITERATURE
IS TO BE PLACED HEREIN.
So I wrote a poem
and popped it in.

Christopher Logue was born in 1926. Educated at Portsmouth Grammar School, he then served as a private in the Black Watch followed by sixteen months in an army prison. His publications include *War Music*, a strikingly original adaption of books 1–4 and 16–19 of Homer's *Iliad*.

Incident in Chapel Market
BY *Barry Cole*

Our attention was at first attracted
When she slipped to the littered ground. The lid
From a sauce bottle escaped beneath the racked
Wood of the nearest stall. Most of us watched.
We wondered what she'd do next, if she would
Raise, collect the packages, the fractured
Jars. None of us moved. We were unprepared
But not, having had time to think, alarmed

When she pressed the kitchen knife to her head
And peeled back the fine skin. In what she did
Was a grace not seen in the retelling. Mad!
Cried a stallholder, zigzaging the packed
Streets for a doctor. But most of us told
Newspapermen precisely what had happened.

This d-stopped sonnet comes from Barry Cole's first full collection, *Moonsearch* (1968). His *Inside Outside – New and Selected Poems* was published in 1997. His latest collection is *Ghosts are People Too* (2003). He has also published four novels. For the past forty-five years he has lived near the Angel, Islington.

Bar Italia
BY *Hugo Williams*

How beautiful it would be to wait for you again
In the usual place,
Not looking at the door,
Keeping a lookout in the long mirror,
Knowing that if you are late
It will not be too late,
Knowing that all I have to do
Is wait a little longer
And you will be pushing through the other customers,
Out of breath, apologetic.
Where have you been, for God's sake?
I was starting to worry.

How long did we say we would wait
If one of us was held up?
It's been so long and still no sign of you.
As time goes by, I search other faces in the bar,
Rearranging their features
Until they are monstrous versions of you,
Their heads wobbling from side to side
Like heads on sticks.
Your absence inches forward
Until it is standing next to me.
Now it has taken the seat I was saving.
Now we are face to face in the long mirror.

Hugo Williams was born in 1942, the son of Hugh Williams, one of the charismatic actors who have recurrently dominated the London stage. Hugo grew up in Sussex and worked on the *London Magazine* from 1961 to 1970, since when he has earned his living as a journalist and travel writer.

Lonely Hearts BY *Wendy Cope*

Can someone make my simple wish come true?
Male biker seeks female for touring fun.
Do you live in North London? Is it you?

Gay vegetarian whose friends are few,
I'm into music, Shakespeare and the sun.
Can someone make my simple wish come true?

Executive in search of something new –
Perhaps bisexual woman, arty, young.
Do you live in North London? Is it you?

Successful, straight and solvent? I am too –
Attractive Jewish lady with a son.
Can someone make my simple wish come true?

I'm Libran, inexperienced and blue –
Need slim non-smoker, under twenty-one.
Do you live in North London? Is it you?

Please write (with photo) to Box 152.
Who knows where it may lead once we've begun?
Can someone make my simple wish come true?
Do you live in North London? Is it you?

Wendy Cope is funny, candid and sometimes erotic, though best
known for her send-ups of contemporary writers. She has been
saluted as the most accomplished living parodist in English
verse.

Photo in St James's Park BY *John Hegley*

a hot spring day by the lake
and a young woman and man
probably tourists
possibly Spanish
who wanted a photo of themselves together
handed their camera to someone
almost definitely English
who certain fellow countrymen
might predictably describe
as a very drunken old dosser
but to them he was just a passer by
he accepted the camera
took a long time focusing
and steadying himself
but managed to take the picture
and received genuine gratitude
from the two
who had seen nothing
deviant in his behaviour
and who would remember him
as a friendly and helpful
English gentleman
if he hadn't fallen in the lake
with their camera

John Hegley was born in 1953 in Newington Green, Islington but moved to Luton while still incontinent. He got a degree in European Literature and the History of Ideas and Sociology which prepared him for working in a children's theatre and at a late-night comedy venue.

Erratum BY Michael Donaghy

I touch the cold flesh of a god in the V and A,
the guard asleep in his chair, and I'm shocked
to find its plaster. These are the reproduction rooms,
where the David stands side by side with the Moses
and Trajan's column (in two halves).
It reminds me of the inventory sequence in *Citizen Kane*.
It reminds me of an evening twenty years ago.

And all at once I'm there, at her side,
turning the pages as she plays
from the yellowed song sheets I rescued from a bookstall:
Dodd's setting of *Antony and Cleopatra*. All very improving.
'Give me my robe and crown' she warbles
in a Victorian coloratura. 'I have immoral longings in me.'

I want to correct her - the word on the page is
immortal - but I'm fourteen and scandalized.
(I knew there were no innocent mistakes.
I'd finished *Modern Masters: Freud*
before she snatched and burned it. 'Filth' –
yanking each signature free of the spine,
'Filth. Filth. Filth.')

The song is over. But when she smiles at me,
I'm on the verge of tears, staring down at the gap-
toothed grimace of our old Bechstein. 'What's wrong?'
What's *wrong*? I check the word again. She's right. Immoral.
She shows me the printer's slip, infecting
the back page of every copy, like,
she might have said, the first sin.

The guard snorts in his dream. I take my palm away
still cool from what I'd taken to be marble.
And when I get the moment back, it's later;
I'm sobbing on her shoulder and I can't say why.
So she suggests another visit to the furnace, where,
to comfort me, perhaps, we rake the cinders with the music
till they chink and spark, and shove the pages
straight into the white core to watch them darken as if ageing,
blacken, enfold, like a sped-up film of blossoms in reverse.

Michael Donaghy, 'the modern metaphysical poet', was born in
the Bronx, New York in 1954. In 1985 he moved to London where
he worked as a teacher and musician until his death in 2004.

London Nautical BY Alan Jenkins

Thamesis suos ubique feret

The boys at my school always used their fists
In bare-knuckle fights behind the boat-sheds,
Smoked and talked about 'bunk-ups' in the bog (or 'heads').
Their taxi-driver dads might as well be Communists,
My dad said, since their strikes had closed the docks.
They came from 'down the Old Kent Road', 'down Vauxhall',
They shouted songs with thrilling words, grabbed their cocks
And mimed tossing off up the changing-room wall . . .
They scared me. I stood to attention, stood at ease
When I was told. I didn't know that I was middle-class
Or that 'sailor' meant you took it up the arse.
They told me I spoke posh so I dropped my tees

And aitches, picked up a glottal stop – a case
Of learn or die. Of saving half my face.

Winter mornings, we chipped ice from the oars
and pulled big whalers round an oil-rainbowed dock.
Upright in the stem, Captain Harding-Raynes
blew thick funnels-full of pipe-smoke,
growled his commands. *Nice weather for chilblains.*
A freezing force-five whipped both shores . . .
Back in the chart-room we pored over azimuths.
We tied one matelot to a chair and hoisted him
with block-and-tackle to the ceiling-pipes;
our marlin-spikes flashed as we spliced wire ropes.
Here are the sails that you will learn to trim.
This is the binnacle, and this the compass.
You will learn to spit and swear and make a rumpus,
you will learn our lovely, nautical, national myths.

England expects . . . – Two months before the mast
on the training ship *Winston Churchill*. I should be proud,
proud as my father was; to turn it down would be immoral,
was the Captain's view. But such was the integrity of our quarrel,
I had so taken to heart, first the sinking in *Lord Jim*
(the film), then *Lord of the Flies*, that I felt miscast,
convinced I was less Ralph than Piggy, that I'd become him
the moment I started wearing my own specs . . .
A three-master under full sail on the open seas!
A crew of strangers, and me, scrubbing decks,
clinging in the topgallant shrouds! I couldn't give it headroom.
Friggin' in the rigging . . . I retreated to my bedroom
and turned the volume on my little mono up to LOUD
for 'Bell-Bottom Blues' or 'Tales of Brave Ulysses'.

While my father sat downstairs and read *Lord Jim*
I toiled at mysteries, dead-reckoning, latitude
and longitude; I buffed my shoes for starboard watch,
saluted on parade and earned the two green stripes
my mother sewed on my uniform. I was living out his hopes,
although we both knew I would never go to sea.
I could hear Harding-Raynes grunting in the ward-room,
could hear his *Huumph. What sort of attitude
does he call that?* And he was right, what with Sandra's crotch,
sea-salty, sultry, luxuriant as the Malayas
that rotted Jim, the twitching exquisite who haunted me,
paralysed with fear while drowning extras thrashed the foam.
Coward. In the heads, hand cupped round a Players
No. 6, I knew what longing was. For her. For home.

From *The Drift* published by Chatto & Windus. Alan Jenkins has published six books of poetry: *In the Hot-house* (1988), *Green Heart* (1990), *Harm* (1994), *The Drift* (2000), *The Little Black Book* (2001) and, in the USA, *A Short History of Snakes* (Selected Poems), also in 2001. He lives in London and is Deputy Editor of the *TLS*.

Previously on 'London Ways'
BY *Edward Barker*

The corrupt doctors' deflowered
An orphan in borough care,
And Mico the hack's been discovered
Taking tenners from his bosses wallet.

Doria the call girl's implant
Complications are, thank god, no
Longer life threatening.
And her arresting detective,
Who gets counselled for his spotted dick
Has brought her flowers, leaving
An emotional question mark floating
Like a circus balloon tied
To the foot of her bed.
Middle class Mary's affair
With the tall south American
junkie painter
who looks like a Californian Jesus has
reached a crisis point:
as proof of her love he's insisting
she share the needle from his arm
early one afternoon before
she picks up her eight
year old twins from school.
So far that's the situation so far.
Next week as promised there's more.

Edward Barker was born in Rome in 1960, the son of the English poet George Barker and the American Lavinia Farelly. He has worked as an actor, a translator and a coordinator for the homeless in Notting Hill where he now lives.

Schmaltz BY *Henry Shukman*

Chicken soup is magic, here's the proof.
Maybe if I'd opened the window a crack
it never would have happened. But late
in the war, I tip the lid to let the steam off

while the broth reduces to clear gold.
Here's my stove up one end and on the table
at the other there's the new baby, the seventh,
the one we didn't want but he was a boy,

after six girls you don't complain.
There's no place for a baby like a warm kitchen,
plus he's wrapped in my husband's
army coat, a proper little bundle.

The Germans find our house by mistake,
drop one right through the roof.
It's the new kind that drips and where it drips
it burns. The girls are all up the road thank god

at their auntie's. I dash into the kitchen,
find a sight. Shouldn't have left the stove,
is my first thought. The room's that smoky
I didn't see the fire was up the other end.

Put my hand straight in the flame.
There he is, snug in his basket, snug all right,
not a squeak or whimper from him,
I don't stop to think what that means.

I pull him out and make for the door.
Outside, I hold him away to get a look

and my whole front's stained with grease.
I wipe his cheek, the skin smooth as ever.

Even with our house pouring smoke behind me,
a tower of flame roaring from the roof,
I can smell what it is on him: schmaltz.
While the room filled with fire he'd been anointed,

and it saved him. No one explained it.
Even the doctor couldn't understand.
He's a plump man our Ruby, always has been,
and loves a bowl of chicken soup with matzoh,

I got some ready whenever he comes.
Oh mom, he says, not chicken soup again;
he's only joking. Yes it is, you ought to know
what's good for you. He's an accountant,

offices off Regent's Park, drives a BMW
just like half his sisters, the ones that didn't
throw themselves away. Wanted to be a fireman
but wasn't tall enough. Changed his name though.

Cohen to Owen. Says it helps in today's Britain.
I'm running out of breath, all this talking,
what I'm saying is, I had a miracle in my life,
never underestimate a good bowl of soup.

Henry Shukman has worked as a trombonist, a trawlerman and
a travel writer, and writes for the *New York Times Book Review*.

Perhaps You Have Dreams
BY *John Stammers*

Perhaps you have dreams of a flat in Hampstead,
of a box at the opera each weekend,
of buying candelabras and dinner parties you'd attend.

I have, for my sins, been a denizen of a West Heath pad,
seen any number of Mimis fall dead,
eaten by candlelight something light on a something green bed.

Perhaps all dreams are what someone who wants you has had
and, not being able to have you, has had what you wanted
                                                    instead.

Taken from John Stammers's *The Panoramic Lounge Bar* published by Picador in 2001; a 'louche and lush collection lit by black humour and bright cinematic touches'.

The Deterioration of Dignity
BY David Robilliard

A tube ride to another boring day's work
every single person in the carriage
has a watch on but me
I can't see the time on any of them
I hate early morning hurries
10 to 9
10 to grind
my mind wanders as we drive along
sitting sideways most of us
the beauty I can see
but not hold
is the same as fool's gold
a shared look goes deeper
than any clever magazine or book
meanwhile in the desert
they are groaning and dying
in their millions in the African plains

David Robilliard was born in Guernsey in 1952 and lived in London for twelve years before his death in 1988. He was celebrated by the artists Gilbert and George who described him as 'the new master of the living person. Looking, thinking, feeling, seeing, bitching – he brilliantly encapsulates the "Existers" spirit of our time'.

Wapping Old Stairs

ANONYMOUS

Your Molly has never been false, she declares,
Since the last time we parted at Wapping Old Stairs;
When I said that I would continue the same,
And I gave you the 'bacco-box marked with my name.
When I passed a whole fortnight between decks with you,
Did I e'er give a kiss, Tom, to one of your crew?
To be useful and kind to my Thomas I stay'd,
For his trousers I washed, and his grog too I made.

Though you promised last Sunday to walk in the Mall
With Susan from Deptford and likewise with Sall,
In silence I stood your unkindness to hear
And only upbraided my Tom with a tear.
Why should Sall, or should Susan, than me be more prized?
For the heart that is true, Tom, should ne'er be despised;
Then be constant and kind, nor your Molly forsake,
Still your trousers I'll wash and your grog too I'll make.

On Shepherd's Bush Roundabout
BY *Gabriel Brown*

The ceaseless burble of
Roundabout living
Is a comforting thing:
Out of reach
Of our each
Neurosea.

Gabriel Brown is the author of *The Adventures of B*, an unpublished novel recounting the sordid obsessions and vices of an unemployed twenty-something. He was born in Hammersmith in 1969, the son of a company secretary and a half-Indian mother. Having graduated from Cambridge he studied Law at Westminster University.

The London Breed BY *Benjamin Zephaniah*

I love dis great polluted place
Where pop stars come to live their dreams
Here ravers come for drum and bass
And politicians plan their schemes,
The music of the world is here
Dis city can play any song
They came to here from everywhere
Tis they that made dis city strong.

A world of food displayed on streets
Where all the world can come and dine
On meals that end with bitter sweets
And cultures melt and intertwine,
Two hundred languages give voice
To fifteen thousand changing years
And all religions can rejoice
With exiled souls and pioneers.

I love dis overcrowded place
Where old buildings mark men and time
And new buildings all seem to race
Up to a cloudy dank skyline,

Too many cars mean dire air
Too many guns mean danger
Too many drugs mean be aware
Of strange gifts from a stranger.

It's so cool when the heat is on
And when it's cool it's so wicked
We just keep melting into one
Just like the tribes before us did,
I love dis concrete jungle still
With all its sirens and its speed
The people here united will
Create a kind of London breed.

From *Too Black, Too Strong* first published by Bloodaxe Books in 2001. *The London Breed* was commissioned by The Museum of London. Benjamin Zephaniah writes, 'The more I travel, the more I love Britain . . . It is probably one of the only places that could take an angry, illiterate, uneducated, ex-hustler, rebellious Rastafarian and give him the opportunity to represent his country . . .'

Acknowledgements

Every effort has been made to trace the holders of copyright and to acknowledge the permission of author and publisher where necessary. If we have inadvertently failed in this mission, we will be pleased to correct any omissions in future editions. Similarly if any reader, translator or poet feels that we have overlooked a favourite verse we would like to hear from them and consider it for inclusion in any subsequent editions.

For 'In Westminster Abbey', 'Slough', 'Monodony on the Death of Aldersgate Street Station' by John Betjeman from his *Collected Poems*. Reprinted by permission of John Murray.

For 'The Garret' and 'The Garden' by Ezra Pound. Reprinted by permission of Faber & Faber.

For 'London Nautical' in *The Drift* by Alan Jenkins, published by Chatto & Windus. Reprinted by kind permission of the Random House Group Ltd.

For 'London Revisited', reprinted by kind permission of Dr Kathleen Raine, C.B.E., the founder of the Temenos Academy.

For 'Perhaps' from *The Panoramic Lounge Bar* by John Stammers published by Picador in 2002. Reprinted by kind permission of Pan Macmillan.

For 'Erratum' in *Dances Learned Last Night: Poems 1975–1995* by Michael Donaghy, published by Picador. Reprinted by kind permission of Pan Macmillan.

For 'Bar Italia' by Hugo Williams, published by Faber & Faber. Reprinted by kind permission of the author and publisher.

For 'Photo in St James's Park' by John Hegley. Reprinted by kind permission of the Carlton Publishing Group.

For 'Schmaltz' from *In Doctor No's Garden* by Henry Shukman, published by Jonathan Cape, part of Random House. Reprinted by kind permission of the author.

For 'Previously by "London Ways"' by Edward Barker. Reprinted by kind permission of the author.

For 'Incident in Chapel Market' from the collection *Inside Outside; New and Selected Poems* by Barry Cole, published by Shoestring Press. Reprinted by kind permission of the author.

For 'On Shepherd's Bush Roundabout' from *A selection of poems* by Gabriel Brown, by kind permission of the author and his agent Rodolph de Salis.

For 'The London Breed' by Benjamin Zephaniah from the Bloodaxe edition *Too Black, Too Strong* (2001) by kind permission of the author and publisher.

Index of First Lines

Index of Poem Titles

143